THE WORLD WHEELCHAIR TRAVELLER

A comprehensive guide for disabled people to get about at home and abroad

by
Susan Abbott
and
Mary Ann Tyrrell

Illustrations by Larry

Foreword
by
Her Royal Highness The Princess Royal

The Spinal Injuries Association is the national voluntary organisation of spinal cord injured people. It has a wide range of appropriate services aimed at enabling even severely disabled people to lead an independent life. ***The World Wheelchair Traveller*** is the latest of its publications.

Susan Abbott is spinal cord injured and, since becoming a wheelchair user, has travelled extensively. She has wide experience of travel facilities for disabled people and is currently an independent travel consultant and UK agent for a holiday complex for disabled people in the Canary Islands.

Mary Ann Tyrrell is General Secretary of the Spinal Injuries Association and Editor of its quarterly journal. Her daily contact with disabled people through the SIA's Information Service and holiday facilities keeps her constantly informed of the travel needs of disabled people. She is currently studying for a degree with the University of London.

Born in 1927, Terence Parkes, better known simply as 'Larry', sold his first cartoon to ***Punch*** in 1953. Nearly 40 years later he remains a regular contributor, as well as to ***Private Eye*** and several of the daily newspapers. Admirers of his loose-lined, apparently effortless style include Alan Coren and Sir Hugh Casson. Larry has published books of his cartoons both in the UK and the USA.

Produced by the Publishing Division of The Automobile Association,
Fanum House, Basingstoke, Hampshire RG21 2EA

Copy Editor: Donna Wood

Printed and bound by BPCC Weatons Ltd, Exeter, Devon

Cover Repro by BTB Reprographics, Whitchurch, Hampshire

A CIP catalogue record of this book is available in the British Library.

ISBN 0 7495 0158 8

Published by The Automobile Association
for the Spinal Injuries Association,
76 St James's Lane, London N10 3DF

The Publishers and the Spinal Injuries Association wish to thank Sir Peter Baldwin, Vice-Chairman of the Committee of The Automobile Association, for his help in making this book possible.

· Foreword ·
by

HRH THE PRINCESS ROYAL

Patron of the Spinal Injuries Association

BUCKINGHAM PALACE

For many able-bodied people the prospect of travel can be daunting as well as challenging, for disabled people - particularly newly disabled people - the prospect can be worse than daunting and an unacceptable challenge.

It is for this reason that I welcome the opportunity to introduce this book since it contains a wealth of experience and information for disabled travellers. The Spinal Injuries Association, of which I am Patron, has produced its new publication by drawing on the experiences of spinal cord injured members - the majority of whom are wheelchair users. Thus the ideas and information contained in these pages come directly from disabled travellers and will, I am sure, prove invaluable to all those who thought that the onset of disability could mean an end to the practicality of travel.

In its daily work the Spinal Injuries Association strives to improve the quality of life of its disabled members and their families. Its new publication will offer new opportunities for travel and enjoyment, something that we able-bodied people take so much for granted.

Anne

· CONTENTS ·

THE WORLD WHEELCHAIR TRAVELLER

So you want to travel the world in your wheelchair......good, then this book is for you! Whether you have only recently injured your spinal cord or if you have been disabled for some time, whether you intend to holiday in the United Kingdom or abroad, if you will be going with family or friends or travelling on your own, you will need to make plans and do your groundwork before you go. That is where this book can help - by pointing you in the right direction for the information you need, and by giving practical tips and advice to ensure a trouble-free trip.

The aim of this book is not to list details of hotels or holiday resorts that are accessible to wheelchair users; this type of information can be obtained from the Spinal Injuries Association Information Service. It is to explain just how to go about making your travel arrangements; what is involved when you book a flight, a ferry or a train; where you can get insurance cover; what type of medical help is available in various countries should you need it; what to do in emergencies; and much, much more. ***The World Wheelchair Traveller*** takes you step-by-step through your travel arrangements, from choosing your luggage to booking a flight, from coping on a long distance flight to getting help abroad, should you need it.

We hope this book will reassure newly injured people that their disability will not prevent them from travelling abroad if they want to, and encourage people with spinal cord injuries (and indeed those with other physical disabilities) who have not so far ventured further than the White Cliffs of Dover to do just that.

There's a whole world out there. ***The World Wheelchair Traveller*** will help you explore it!

THE SPINAL INJURIES ASSOCIATION

SIA is the leading national organisation of and for spinal cord injured people in the UK. Among its aims is the desire to see disabled people fully integrated into all activities of daily life, whether it be employment, travel, family life or career. In fact, whatever lifestyle the disabled person chooses, the Spinal Injuries Association is there to assist him or her in achieving it.

The Association, founded in 1974 and with HRH the Princess Royal as its Patron, is run by spinal cord injured people who have a wealth of expertise upon which to draw. The ever-growing membership is actively involved in identifying the needs of spinal cord injured people. In response SIA has designed and implemented a variety of services. These ensure that those who become paralysed through damage to the spinal cord, whether by accident or illness, have every opportunity to experience and enjoy life to the full once more.

SIA's services include assistance on welfare matters, family support, information on all aspects of daily living (from choosing the right wheelchair to how to keep fit and healthy after paralysis), support with personal care needs, producing publications about living with spinal cord injury, providing holidays in specially designed facilities (including two narrow boats) and publishing a lively quarterly journal packed with news and views on the world of spinal cord injury.

Membership of the Spinal Injuries Association is open to all. For a free Information Pack contact:

General Secretary
Spinal Injuries Association
Newpoint House
76 St James's Lane
Muswell Hill
London N10 3DF
Tel: 081-444 2121

CHAPTER ONE

MAKING PLANS

CHOOSING A TRAVEL AGENT

Once you have decided that you want or need a break, you will have to choose your destination and decide how you will travel and spend your time. For example, do you want the convenience of using a travel agent to make your arrangements for you, or would you prefer to make your own travel plans, choosing certain routes for added flexibility? Some disabled people - perhaps those who live alone or need personal care - may well prefer to holiday with a group of others for company and/or support.

Local travel agents

If you intend to do a lot of travelling always try your local travel agent first for advice and information. You may have to begin by explaining about the effects of spinal cord injury, or the disability you have, but once made aware of your needs, an agent can take most of the slog out of booking and make all the necessary arrangements for you.

Be accurate about your requirements and the facilities you are looking for on holiday.

It may be a good idea to provide the travel agent with a checklist of the sort of facilities you are likely to need. This could include:

- accessible transport to and from your home to your holiday destination or airport
- assistance at the airport and help boarding the plane
- accessible accommodation, including ramped or level access, parking, details of the size of lifts and width of all doors, accessible toilet and bathroom, manoeuvrability of wheelchair in rooms, position of toilet in bathroom for easy transfer, height of bed, access to balcony, accessibility of kitchen if self-catering
- access to local amenities, transport, shops, entertainments, beach, places of interest.

Give your travel agent a copy of SIA's holiday questionnaire, so that the relevant details can be filled in for you before you go. You could then compare two or three hotels and choose the most convenient. Let the agent know the width of your wheelchair in centimetres if you are travelling abroad, (a standard manual is 26in wide, which converts to 66cm) and of any special diets or services you may need while away from home.

Make sure the travel agent you choose is an ABTA member in case of subsequent difficulties. ABTA has a free Conciliation Service to settle any disputes and issues a leaflet *How ABTA Safeguards your Holiday* obtainable from travel agents who are ABTA members or from the Association of British Travel Agents. ABTA has also produced a leaflet *How to help the Disabled Traveller* which is primarily aimed at the commercial holiday companies, to help them to assist any of their clients who may be physically disabled. Make sure that your travel agent has given prior notification to the hotel manager at your destination and other authorities who will be assisting you, such as airport, ferry, coach or rail station personnel.

Make sure couriers arranging transfers between airport and hotel are aware of your disability, so that alternative transport can be arranged if necessary. The majority of commercial tour operators use a standard coach or minibus for transfers between point of arrival and hotel. If you cannot negotiate steps it may be better to use a local taxi if the journey is a short one. If it is a long journey you will need to arrange with the travel agent or tour operator to have someone available to assist you on to the coach.

Financial Help To Go On Holiday

Under the Chronically Sick and Disabled Persons Act 1970, local authorities have a duty to assess the needs of disabled people and the services they require. The need for a holiday is included in these services and you are entitled to approach your local social services department to see if they can help with a grant towards the cost of your holiday, whether in the UK or abroad. Generally, holiday grants are quite small, but some local authorities are more generous than others, so it is always worth a try.

If you are an SIA member, the Association may be able to help you by contacting grant-making trusts or benevolent organisations on your behalf from the Directory of Grant Making Trusts.

Handicapped Aid Trust provides financial assistance for severely disabled people travelling abroad who need to take a personal care attendant/helper with them, but cannot afford to do so.

The Trust also collects small change in foreign currency from returning holidaymakers in order to finance the scheme. So, if you are returning home with a pocketful of pesetas these could help a severely disabled person to enjoy a foreign holiday.

Application form from The Secretary, 21 Malden Hill, New Malden, Surrey KT3 4DS.

Holiday Care Service provides information on possible sources of finance towards holidays for people in need. Most of the trusts and benevolent funds on their list require an application to be made by an official body, such as a local authority or health service, and will not accept applications from individuals.

Local voluntary organisations such as the Lions, Round Table, Rotary Club etc, are often willing to give financial help to disabled travellers who have the motivation but lack the means. Contact your local Association of Voluntary Services for names and addresses.

National voluntary organisations who arrange holidays abroad, such as the Winged Fellowship Trust Holidays Overseas and Mobility International may also be able to give advice on ways of offsetting the cost of your foreign holiday, either for yourself or your helper.

Package Tours

Many SIA members use established commercial package holidays, some of which cater in a modest way for disabled travellers. Many leading tour operators now give more thought to the needs of disabled holidaymakers than in the past and will advise on the suitability of accommodation and facilities used on their package holidays, as well as providing useful details about the surrounding area. However, information gleaned over the telephone often leads to disappointment, so always double-check by writing to the operators explaining your requirements in full. This should avoid being confronted by a flight of steps into a holiday hotel which you had been told was all on the level.

The following are some of the leading package tour operators who run hotel and self-catering holidays in Europe and world wide and can advise disabled travellers.

Thomsons Holidays has collaborated with the Holiday Care Service to gather information about accommodation accessibility and suitability of the surrounding area. Thomsons also say their staff are trained to be aware of the requirements of people with disabilities. Thomsons' brochure states they want to make it easy for everyone to go on holiday, regardless of limited mobility and suggest you call their Client Services department for advice on accessible accommodation and travel arrangements. They are happy to carry collapsible wheelchairs on their flights.

Horizon Holidays has a list of hotels which they consider suitable for use by disabled people. Decide upon the resort you wish to visit and they will advise which hotels are suitable for your needs, as they hold details about accessibility and suitability of all their hotels on file. Horizon's representatives have checked suitable hotels and taken measurements of doors, number of steps, etc, but stress that none of their hotels have been specially adapted in any way for disabled people. Horizon will make all the necessary flight arrangements if you are in a wheelchair.

Sovereign/Enterprise Holidays (British Airways Tour Operator), holds a list of hotels which they consider suitable for use by disabled people. First choose the resort and they will advise on accommodation. Their representatives fill out questionnaires on all the hotels used in their brochures, including access details for disabled clients. Sovereign will also make all the necessary arrangements for the flight.

Cosmos has brief details on each hotel and can advise as to their suitability. Their operations department will liaise with the airport concerned to make all the necessary flight arrangements.

Thomas Cook Holidays holds a list on computer of all the accessible hotels they use in their brochures and are happy to advise disabled clients and make all the necessary arrangements. Other tour operators who will help disabled clients to find suitable holiday accommodation are ***Wings***, **OSL** who have details of some self-catering holiday villas which may be suitable, ***Eurocamp*** and ***Carefree Camping***, who indicate which of their ready-erected tent campsite venues are suitable by using the international access symbol. ***Golden Rail Holidays*** also use the international access symbol in their brochures (available from British Rail Travel Centres) to indicate those hotels which are suitable for disabled travellers. ***Lanzarote Villas*** will, on request, mark suitable villas in their brochure and ***Meon Villa Holidays*** can advise on self-catering villas in Portugal. Hafod Wen, which was purpose-built by a disabled owner, can be booked through them. ***Vacances Franco-Britanniques*** use the wheelchair symbol in their brochures as an indication to disabled people.

The international access symbol used in holiday brochures should only be taken as a very broad guide and not a guarantee that you will find completely suitable accommodation and accessible facilities at your holiday destination.

Details of all European hotel accommodation is listed in the Independent Hotel Gazetteer, which all tour operators and travel agents have access to and they can check accommodation details in it for you. So ask your travel agent to look up a specific hotel if you are unsure of what is on offer.

The Holiday Care Service can supply a list of package tour operators who have information to help a disabled

holidaymaker plan a holiday abroad. It can also supply a list of overseas holiday accommodation visited and inspected by them. This covers popular Mediterranean holiday resorts, their suitability for wheelchair users and other disabled travellers, and an access summary of the hotels used in those resorts. Sadly, most of the hotels inspected have flights of steps to the entrance, narrow lift doors and even narrower bathroom doors in their bedrooms.

But do not despair! The Spinal Injuries Association has details of hotels and self-catering accommodation tried and tested by wheelchair users and there are a number of useful publications you can consult. The AA ***Guide for the Disabled Traveller*** contains a wide range of travel and holiday information. Comprehensive details of access are given.

The RADAR Guide ***Holidays & Travel Abroad - Guide for Disabled People*** which is updated annually and is available from RADAR or large high street bookshops, contains useful information and lists accommodation which may be suitable for a disabled holidaymaker (but has not necessarily been personally inspected by a wheelchair user). It is essential, therefore, that you are completely satisfied that the accommodation and resort you have selected meets all your requirements before booking.

Package tours are usually cheaper than booking flights and accommodation through your travel agent, but it is not so easy to check all the specific details. Aircraft and hotels used by package tour operators are usually more cramped and crowded as the object is to pack in as many people as possible. However, many of our members report having had successful holidays with package tour operators.

HOLIDAYS IN THE UK

Voluntary Organisations

The Spinal Injuries Association has a great deal of information on interesting and accessible holiday accommodation which has been used by members. The accommodation covers all types of holidays - self catering, hotels, holiday camps and camping holidays. In addition to this, SIA also has its own mobile homes in Sussex, Yorkshire and France and two specially designed narrow boats for use by its members. These highly popular facilities, which are completely wheelchair accessible, can be booked through the SIA office.

The RADAR guide ***Holidays for Disabled People*** and the Holiday Care Service both provide information about the accessibility and facilities of all types of holiday accommodation to help disabled people find something suitable. The Holiday Care Service has over 240 different information sheets on resorts and holiday accommodation, though even with tried and tested accommodation, always check that it meets your specific requirements before booking.

A number of disability organisations own accessible and adapted holiday accommodation that they rent to members and non-members. Details of these can be obtained from a RADAR fact sheet and the Holiday Care Service.

Commercial Organisations

Some commercial organisations can, to some extent, cater for disabled holiday makers and it is always worth enquiring to see if the facilities might be suitable.

Blakes Holidays, who are booking agents for self-catering holiday homes and also offer boating holidays, can advise on which they consider suitable for use by disabled people.

Both ***Butlins*** and ***Pontins*** holiday centres have some special adaptations for disabled people at some of their centres, but it is essential to check with their head office that you can comfortably use all facilities before you go.

Country Farm Holidays offer self-catering accommodation and can indicate which of their properties are suitable for disabled people. ***Country Holidays***, the largest cottage holiday rental company in the UK, has set up a special department, with a trained adviser, to arrange self-catering holidays for people with disabilities.

However, always double-check with your travel agent or tour operator about accommodation and facilities and be sure they know your exact requirements, especially if you are a wheelchair user.

Some hotel chains do offer accommodation, both in the UK and abroad, with provision for disabled travellers. Some have specially designed bedrooms with adapted bathrooms which wheelchair travellers can use without too much trouble. This type of hotel can often be fairly luxurious and, therefore, expensive, but before you write them off on that basis, inquire if they operate weekend out-of-season breaks; many of them offer two or three day 'special breaks' at reduced prices. Some hotel companies issue brochures, most of which use the international access symbol.

This book lists some hotel chains operating special breaks, and further advice can be sought direct from their head offices - Best Western Hotels, Crest Hotels, Holiday Inns, Ibis, Urbis Hotels, Marriott Hotels, Novotel and Sofitel Hotels, Ramada Hotels and Sheraton Hotels. In addition to these, Little Chef has motel accommodation which in some cases is suitable for disabled travellers. The Higher Education Accommodation Consortium can advise on which colleges and polytechnics have holiday accommodation suitable for disabled people available during vacation time. An advantage to some is that this type of institution often has single rooms to offer for those who do not want to share.

Another source of accessible hotel accommodation is the English Tourist Board, which updates and issues annually a number of publications using the international access symbol to denote that accommodation may be suitable for disabled people.

The three guides that use the access symbol where appropriate are ***Hotels, Guesthouses and Universities***, ***Farmhouses and Bed and Breakfast*** and ***Holiday Homes and Holiday Centres***. These are available from Department D, English Tourist Board, 4 Bromells Road, London SW4 0BJ. Always double-check that the accommodation and facilities are what you are looking for because they are not inspected and there can be a wealth of difference between what a hotel proprieter or bed and breakfast landlady thinks a wheelchair user wants and what he or she actually needs.

The publications mentioned above are all inexpensive. The English Tourist Board also publishes annually and free of charge ***Let's Go***, which lists two and three-day holiday breaks offered at hotels throughout England. The Wales Tourist Board publishes its own ***Disabled Visitors' Guide to Wales*** which is updated annually and covers accommodation considered suitable for disabled people as well as information on places to visit and, most essential, accessible toilet facilities. The Northern Ireland Tourist Board publishes a booklet called ***The Disabled Tourist in Northern Ireland - Things to See, Places to Stay*** plus ***Northern Ireland: All the Places to Stay***, which uses the access symbol. The Scottish Tourist Board issues ***Scotland - 1001 Things to See, Where to Stay***, and ***Events in Scotland***, all of which give information on accommodation, places to visit and access for disabled visitors. Information on accessible holiday accommodation is available from the Scottish Council on Disability who publish a list annually and can help with holiday queries from disabled holidaymakers. The AA publishes the excellent ***Guide for the Disabled Traveller***.

Guide - Lecture Service

In 1981 William Forester, an SIA member, became the first Guide in a wheelchair to be registered with the London Tourist Board. Since then he has qualified as a City of London Guide, a Cumbria Guide and a Round Britain Tour Escort. An Oxford history graduate and qualified teacher, he works as a guide for the British Museum and as an adult education lecturer for the University of Surrey. William is able to offer his services, based on his own experience, to both individuals and groups whether disabled or able bodied. An important part of his guiding activities is a mini-bus tour service in and around London using wheelchair-accessible transport as well as an itinerary planning service. In 1981 he won the British Tourist Authority Award for outstanding services to disabled visitors and in 1989 became the Tour Guide of the Year, the first time this award has ever been given.

Further enquiries via William Forester, 1 Belvedere Close, Guildford, Surrey GU2 6NP Tel: (0483) 575401.

GOING WITH A GROUP

For some, one of the most pleasurable experiences of travelling and taking a holiday is making new acquaintances. For this reason, travelling with a group of others appeals and where transport, accommodation, outings and volunteer helpers are provided, this type of holiday can take a lot of worry out of travelling for severely disabled people.

Group travel

There are several specialist and group travel organisations, some of which are listed in Chapter 10. Voluntary organisations providing group holidays, such as Winged Fellowship Trust and Young Disabled on Holiday, often provide helpers. PHAB (Physically Handicapped and Able-bodied) organise holidays for mixed groups of physically handicapped and able-bodied people. Many are aimed at children or young people and are often activity holidays or courses. Commercial specialist tour operators do not provide helpers but claim that their holiday accommodation has been inspected for wheelchair accessibility. Others, such as Carefree Holidays, organise group travel for people with special needs and use a coach with a side lift on their tours. They can also lend equipment such as commodes, monkey poles, etc.

There are some helpers on the holiday who assist the group generally, but if you need a personal helper you will have to take your own along with you. Chalfont Line also uses specially designed coaches with

hydraulic lifts for touring. Assistance Travel Service arranges group holidays for individuals and families with a disabled member to Florida and organisations like PHAB and Mobility International offer a range of worldwide destinations. All these companies offer a wide variety of holidays both here in the UK and abroad.

A comprehensive list of specialist organisations involved in group travel for disabled people can be found in ***Holidays in the British Isles, A Guide for Disabled People (UK)*** and ***Holidays and Travel Abroad - Guide for Disabled People***, both published by RADAR or from the Holiday Care Service.

The Holiday Care Service is a central reference point providing free information on all aspects of holidaymaking both in the UK and abroad. However, it is not a booking agency and can only provide you with information and advice. Contact it well in advance of your holiday as it tends to be very busy during the summer months.

GOING IT ALONE

Apart from the extent of their mobility, disabled travellers are no different from any other type of traveller and for this reason many will want to make their own arrangements and not be bound by package tour schedules or the wishes of others. There is no reason at all why, with careful planning, a disabled traveller, even a severely disabled person (perhaps with a care attendant) should not make his or her own arrangements and be free to come and go.

If you intend to make your own travel arrangements allow plenty of time to do as much research as you can. Holiday brochures and travel agencies are a good starting point and will be able to give you information about your holiday destination but to get the full picture, the tourist office of the particular country you want to visit will be able to send you brochures, maps and information leaflets; they may also have specialist information about facilities for disabled visitors. They can tell you what the weather will be like at the time of your visit, whether any special health requirements have to be met, and provide details about places of interest. There is a full list of tourist offices in Chapter 10.

As well as brochures, travel agencies and tourist offices, you should also consult all the guidebooks you can find. Either borrow them from the local public library or buy your own copy from most high street book shops or AA Centres, where there is an extensive range. Some of the better ones are the ***Michelin Green Guides*** and ***Baedeker Guides***, and the newly published ***Essential Guides*** from The Automobile Association, all of which are packed with useful information on a particular country, region or city. They also give useful motoring and travel tips. It may be worth consulting back numbers of ***Holiday Which?***, published by the Consumers' Association. These contain exhaustive surveys of popular holiday destinations and are full of objective information and sensible advice. You can get hold of back numbers of ***Holiday Which?*** from the local reference library as well as the publisher. The reference library may also hold a copy of the Agents' Hotel Gazetteer, and if it does, consult a copy before you go as this will give you valuable information on how accessible the hotel really is, and what facilities it has to offer a disabled guest.

SIA has comprehensive listings of holiday accommodation both in the UK and abroad which has been tried, tested and recommended by its members. The listings include information on hotels, motels, self-catering establishments, caravans, guesthouses and farmhouses, plus details of the surrounding area and places to visit. This will provide you with a solid base for a successful self-start holiday. However, always check that the facilities are suitable for your personal needs. Everyone is different!

For those who are more adventurous there are activity holidays offering orienteering or sailing for example. Some organisations run centres catering exclusively for disabled people and there are holidays for those with a mixture of abilities, including everything from abseiling and archery to canoeing and sailing. If the outdoor life sounds too strenuous then there are specialist centres which are more concerned with broadening the mind than the muscles. Several of these can offer suitable accommodation for disabled people to study anything from archaeology to computer studies or pursue interests such as photography or cake decorating.

There is also valuable guidance on accommodation in the AA's ***Guide for the Disabled Traveller***, published annually.

A list of activity centres for sporting holidays and establishments which offer special interest holidays can be found in the RADAR Guide ***Holidays for Disabled People*** and ***Activity and Hobby Holidays***, available from the English Tourist Board. Some Youth Hostels, both in the UK and abroad, offer accommodation which may be suitable for disabled youth hostellers. ***The International Youth Hostel Handbook*** covers the UK and other countries and uses the international access symbol to denote accessibility.

If you would like to participate in projects which help other people, why not try a Workcamp? It may sound like a sentence to hard labour on a chain-gang, but quite the opposite is true. Disabled people can participate with able-bodied people on a working holiday, run by the International Voluntary Service and Quaker International, who operate Workcamps abroad as well as in the UK.

If a Workcamp doesn't appeal, then there are facilities for wheelchair campers. The organisation Camping for the Disabled can supply information and advice on suitable campsites both at home and in Europe. Some of the Forestry Commission's campsites have facilities for disabled campers and the Forestry Commission issues several free brochures giving details of its sites and forest cabin holiday homes. On some of the sites run by The Camping and Caravan Club there are facilities for disabled campers and the club is happy to supply details of the suitable sites.

If you have chosen a holiday destination abroad, remember that not all hotel proprietors speak perfect English and your letter or telephone call may have been misunderstood (***The Disabled Traveller's International Phrasebrook*** may be useful here). Make sure that your needs will be fully catered for. Try contacting the Tourist Board of the country you intend to visit to see if it can help with correspondence, phone calls etc. Many Tourist Boards produce useful guides on access and accommodation for disabled tourists. Some of the overseas Tourist Boards, such as the Netherlands Board of Tourism, produce excellent and comprehensive information booklets packed with relevant details for the disabled traveller, while others (Greece for example) can produce only a short list of hotels considered suitable. If you are flying to foreign parts for the first time it is worth contacting the Tourist Board of the country you are visiting at its London headquarters even if it only produces general information about the country. Always allow plenty of time to make travel and accommodation reservations. A list of International Tourist Boards appears in Chapter 10.

INTERNATIONAL HOTEL CHAINS

Some hotel chains do make provision for disabled travellers and have specially designed bedrooms with *en suite* bathrooms for wheelchair users. However, they tend to be expensive and, as they are normally sited close to motorways, are intended for a one or two-day stop-over, not a two-week holiday. The majority of the hotel chains use the International Access Symbol in their brochures.

Hotel chains which have accessible accommodation are listed in Chapter 10 and can be booked directly through their UK office, eliminating the need for a phrase book at this stage.

GETTING THERE

Information on all forms of travel to and from your holiday destination appears in later chapters together with tips on going (or not going) to the loo and having a comfortable journey.

PERSONAL ASSISTANCE

If you are not an independent traveller, you will probably venture forth with a friend, relative or your own helper who can provide the assistance you need. If you are spinal cord injured the Spinal Injuries Association can provide a care attendant through its Care Attendant Agency. Be sure to book well in advance because it is a popular and well used service during the summer months. The Holiday Care Service runs a Holiday Helpers Scheme, which puts disabled travellers in touch with volunteer helpers so that they may take a holiday independently of families or organised groups. The Holiday Care Service takes account of the age, experience and interests of both parties. Payment for the helper's accommodation and travel must be arranged between the two people concerned.

Other agencies who may be able to help are Community Service Volunteers, the British Nursing Association or your local nursing agency. You will need to check their charges when booking and take this into account when calculating the overall cost of your holiday.

AIDS AND EQUIPMENT

If you need simple aids on your UK holiday and cannot take your own away with you, contact the Red Cross Society at a branch nearest your holiday destination. It may be able to lend you the necessary equipment. Most overseas countries have a Red Cross Association or similar organisation who can give advice on the hire of aids and equipment.

If you do not like the idea of borrowing medical aids why not invest in some essential equipment that you can use both at home and also take on holiday? Make sure the items you choose are easy to pack or will collapse for transportation, can be cleaned easily, and most important, will not break the bank! You can see equipment at the Disabled Living Foundation if you live near London, and if not, there are several permanent exhibitions around the country where aids can be inspected. Information relating to your nearest Aids Centre can be obtained from the Joint Aid Centres Council. Sometimes your local Disabled Living Centre will hold a small exhibition, or can give you advice on suitability and cost. If you have a sympathetic Social Services Department, your social worker or disabled living adviser may be able to provide essential items and also give you up-to-date information on what is available. The type of aids you may want to think about taking away with you are; a collapsible portable commode in case the bathroom is unsuitable or toilet too low or inaccessible, a set of folding rails which can be a 'life saver' to place around a low toilet; a raised toilet seat and a set of bed blocks to raise a low bed - although if you ask hotel management for another mattress this will raise the bed height for a comfortable transfer. Some disabled people never travel anywhere without their sliding board, and this is particularly useful if you intend to do a lot of sightseeing by taxi.

These are just a few suggestions and obviously you are the best judge of which aids will be a help to you while on holiday and away from home.

Medical equipment may be taken free of charge on aeroplanes and some items (ie incontinence equipment such as a collapsible commode or box of pads) will not be included in baggage weight allowances, but be sure to check with your travel agent, or the airline, before departure.

CHAPTER TWO

DOING THE PAPERWORK

HOLIDAY INSURANCE

The importance of holiday insurance cannot be stressed enough.

If you travel with a package tour operator, your insurance wil probably be included in the price of the holiday, but it is essential to check with the travel agent or, better still, the insurers to see if it covers your 'pre-existing medical condition'. Some SIA members report being refused insurance while other members of the family have been accepted.

Medical expenses abroad can be astronomical, so it is wise to budget for insurance in the price of your holiday. There are now a number of insurance companies who cater specifically for disabled people and include in their cover personal accident, medical expenses, baggage and personal effects, wheelchair indemnity, personal money, personal liability, travel delay, and, most important, holiday cancellation.

All the insurance agencies we list will only give insurance cover to disabled people who are not travelling against medical advice and provided they take enough medication to cover the duration of their holiday. It is very important that sufficient cover is obtained. The names and addresses of insurers are listed at the end of this chapter.

Prices are variable, so shop around for the best bargain. Some people have had experience of their wheelchairs being damaged during their holiday and if you own an expensive private wheelchair, whether electric or manual, it is always best to insure it.

If you are planning a trip to Europe, remember that free or reduced-cost emergency treatment is available in European Community countries if you are suddenly taken ill or have an accident during your visit, provided you have a form called an E111. In an emergency, you would receive care on the same terms as nationals of the country visited, but private treatment is not covered. A list of EEC countries who provide free or reduced-cost treatment can be found in the Department of Health's leaflet SA 40 *Before You Go,* available from your local Department of Health office at least a month before you go, or by ringing Freephone (0800) 555777. You can also obtain a free copy of SA 41 *While You're Away* which contains information about protecting your health abroad and how to cope in an emergency, by ringing the same number. The leaflet takes about a week in the post, so contact your local DoH in good time.

Keep your E111 form in a safe place, preferably with your passport, but bear in mind that the E111 does not cover all medical expenses. It does not, for example, cover the cost of repatriation to the UK in the event of an emergency, or driving accidents in some countries, so always back it up with private insurance.

Europe Assistance Ltd specialises in holiday motor insurance and provides comprehensive protection for the disabled motorist travelling abroad. This can include motoring protection, medical emergency service and personal cover, together with on-the-spot medical help.

'Keep Motoring' AA Insurance scheme for disabled people

This is an insurance scheme which is designed to keep physically disabled motorists on the move when their specially adapted cars have been taken off the road for repair.

Introduced in conjunction with RADAR, the new AA Autoquote motor insurance scheme is aimed primarily at those whose vehicles are converted to hand controls.

It gives disabled motorists the benefits of discounted car hire enjoyed by other drivers insured with the AA, by providing a similarly adapted replacement car within 24 hours of notification, when normally it can take up to a week to obtain a substitute vehicle. The reduced rate also applies if the policyholder's car breaks down and has to go into a garage for repairs, as well as for accident damage attention.

Under the scheme, Hertz RentaCar will supply an automatic 3-door 1.3 Austin Metro to an AA depot convenient to the insured driver, where AA engineers will fit it with a COWAL hand control and a pedal guard. When the car is no longer needed, it can be returned to the nearest Hertz depot for de-fitting.

The insurance package includes hire of the converted vehicle at the lowest tariff rate, unlimited mileage, and a collision damage waiver - equivalent to a discount of more than 50 per cent on normal car-hire rates.

Other benefits included in the AA Autoquote Policy are claims assistance, the use of the AA's unique drive-in assessment centres and free windscreen etching.

The scheme also offers a disabled motorists' Loss of Use Policy to cover the cost of alternative transport; a mechanical breakdown insurance option; and a 10 per cent discount on AA Homesure contents and buildings insurance. A 12.5 per cent discount is available to disabled motorists who also take up AA personal membership, including Relay and Homestart.

Quotations can be obtained at any of the AA Insurance's 160 local offices, or by dialling 100 and asking for Freefone AA Autoquote.

Insurance Companies

The following will provide disabled travellers with insurance cover and make no exclusions for 'pre-existing medical conditions' - provided you are not travelling against medical advice, you are fit enough to travel and take enough medication to cover the duration of your holiday.

- **M J Fish & Co**
  FREEPOST, 1-3 Slater Lane
  Leyland. Preston PR5 3AL
  Tel: (0772) 455111
  specialist insurance brokers for disabled people
- **Extra-Sure Holidays**
  Lloyd's Avenue House
  6 Lloyd's Avenue, London EC3N 3AX
  Tel: 071-488 9341 or Travel Agents registered with ABTA
  Extra Sure Travel Insurance.
  Comprehensive travel cover
- **A M Mars (PG) Ltd**
  Altay House, 869 High Road
  North Finchley, London N12 8QA
  Tel: 081-882 4511
  Travelmarrs' Handicare package. No pre-existing medical conditions, but check details
- **Europe Assistance Ltd**
  252 High Street, Croydon
  Surrey CR0 1NF
  Tel: 081 680 1234
  offers two standard schemes:
  a) personal service covering a full range of medical emergencies
  b) motoring emergencies service caters for the motorist abroad

USEFUL LEAFLETS

SA40 *Before You Go* -Information for people preparing to travel abroad (includes application form to obtain document E111 for medical treatment)

SA 41 *While You're Away* -Information for people travelling abroad (includes information on how to get treratment in other European Community Countries)

NI 38 *Social Security Abroad* -A guide to National Insurance Contributions Benefits outside the European Community

Copies of these leaflets are available from your local Department of Health office or from its Overseas Branch, in Newcastle upon Tyne NE98 1YX. Alternatively dial Freephone (0800) 555777.

Acquiring a Full UK Passport

When you travel abroad there are a number of items you can leave behind without much harm being done, but one thing you MUST have before you travel abroad is your valid passport or British Visitor's passport.

If you already have a passport, check to make sure it is still a current one (full UK passports are valid for 10 years). If it is out of date, have it renewed in plenty of time. It is recommended that you post or take your application to the passport office at least six weeks before you wish to travel. During April to August applications take longer than at other times of the year, so be warned. Get yourself organised well in advance (if any emergency arises, or if you need a passport in less than four weeks, get in touch with your Regional Passport Office, which should be able to rush one through).

To obtain a passport you will need to complete an application form MISC 314 (obtainable by post from passport offices or in person from a post office). Helpful and comprehensive notes are included with the form to help you fill out your application. When you have completed the form you will need to have it countersigned by a professionally qualified person, for example a doctor, engineer, lawyer, teacher, bank manager, established civil servant, police officer or a person of similar standing who has known you personally for at least two years (the work of the passport office includes a check that the countersignature is genuine). A relative should not countersign. The person who countersigns your application will also have to countersign the photographs of yourself which you need to supply. Two identical recent portrait photographs are needed. Family passports are no longer issued, although existing family passports can be used until expiry. Each person over 16 years of age must apply for a separate passport. Children under 16 may be included in parent's passport and their photographs are not required.

When you have completed the application form, have both it and the photographs countersigned. Send them with the necessary original documents which you will need to submit with your application (birth, marriage or naturalisation certificates where appropriate), either by post, or take them to a passport office. When posting, enclose your cheque and write your name and address on the back of the envelope, keeping a note of the EXACT date of posting (this is in case your application goes astray). Remember that taking your application personally to a passport office may mean queueing and does not guarantee priority treatment.

At the time of writing, the fee for a United Kingdom Passport of up to 32 pages, without particulars of wife or husband, is £15. Most people find that a standard passport of 30 pages is adequate. However, for those who travel often a 94-page passport may be preferable.

Incidentally, when you apply for a new passport you must give up any previous passport held.

Your new passport will be sent to you by first class post, but if you want it returned by registered post you will need to send a further fee to cover the cost.

Do keep this valuable document in a safe place. Carry it with you at all times while on holiday and, as an extra precaution in case of loss, keep a separate note of its number and date and place of issue.

British Visitors' Passport

You may, however, prefer just to apply for a British Visitors' Passport if you do not intend to travel a great deal. It is valid for one year only and can be used for holidays or unpaid business trips of up to three months. If you want this type of passport, ask for form MISC 320 from your passport or post office and take the completed form in person to a main post office if you live in England, Wales or Scotland, or to the post office at Hampton House, 47-53 High Street, Belfast, if you live in Northern Ireland. A British Visitors' Passport costs £7.50 (or £11.25 if a spouse is to be included).

VISAS OR PERMITS

It may be that entry into the country you wish to visit will also require a visa or permit. A visa is an authorisation for you to enter and leave a particular country and is usually stamped inside your passport. It gives the length of time you can stay in a country as well as how many times it can be used before it expires. If you are not sure whether the country you wish to visit requires you to have a visa, check with your travel agent or with the Consulate of the country. As with a passport, you will be required to fill out an application form, supply photographs etc. It is a simple procedure but it does take time, so check well in advance if you need a visa and, if you do, allow yourself sufficient time to get one.

CHAPTER THREE

FOREIGN CURRENCY

The old adage 'You can't take it with you when you go' certainly does not apply when travelling abroad - in fact, some countries will not let you in unless you have enough money to see you through your stay and to pay for the return journey.

Decide in good time not only how much money you need to take with you, but in what form. You can choose to take either Travellers' cheques or cash, credit cards or Eurocheques.

TRAVELLERS' CHEQUES

This is one of the safest ways to carry your money while you are travelling, especially if your journey will take you outside Western Europe. You can buy Travellers' cheques at any high street bank regardless of whether you hold an account there or not. Usually there is a small administrative charge levied. Travellers' cheques can be bought in all major currencies (sterling, dollars, French francs, Deutsche marks, Yen, etc) and in a variety of denominations. In the USA, many banks have no facilities for exchanging Travellers' cheques or foreign currency. However, you can use dollar Travellers' cheques just like the Americans do - as cash. You will find you can use them in any shops, hotels, restaurants, and even buses, as if they were actual dollar bills.

If you need Travellers' cheques in a hurry, or at the last minute, do not panic, most airports have an arrangement with the major banks and can provide you with Travellers' cheques in most of the major currencies. You would have to pay for them in cash. Also, most channel ports and cross-channel ferries have a Bureau de Change which you can use, but the rates of exchange may not be as favourable as those found at a bank.

Incidentally, when purchasing Travellers' cheques, most banks provide you with a useful leaflet giving good advice about security and loss of cheques. It is a good idea to keep a note of the numbers of your Travellers' cheques in case you lose them or they are stolen. In fact, when you are issued with Travellers' cheques you will be given a purchase agreement which is, in fact, a receipt and which gives the numbers of the cheques. You should keep this receipt in a separate place to the Travellers' cheques, as it gives the telephone number to call in the unfortunate event of your Travellers' cheques being lost or stolen. This number is normally a 24-hour seven-day a week service and you can call on a reverse charge basis from any part of the world.

CREDIT CARDS

Major credit cards such as Access, American Express and Barclaycard (Visa) are recognised in most countries. However, you would be well advised not to rely on them totally but to carry some other form of currency in addition (this will save you having to do the washing-up in out-of-the-way restaurants where they do not recognise the card!).

If you are considering a visit to the hypermarkets on your journey and intend using your credit card - be warned! Not all hypermarkets accept them and some insist on cash in local currency only.

Charges for a credit card transaction are normally calculated at the rate of exchange on the day the transaction is processed, not on the day it is made. Therefore, as well as allowing for the high interest attracted on credit cards if you do not settle in full on the due day, you need to take account of fluctuating rates of exchange.

If you take your credit cards abroad, keep a note of which ones you take, the account numbers and who to contact if they get lost or stolen - leave a copy of this record at home and take one with you.

EUROCHEQUES

Major banks now issue Eurocheques which you can use in excactly the same way as you use your normal cheques at home - for paying bills, buying goods and services, and for getting cash out of a bank. Eurocheques can be used at almost 200,000 banks and over 4.5 million retailers, restaurants and hotels in 39 European countries and are guaranteed for up to the local equivalent of £100.

With Eurocheques, the money only comes out of your personal cheque account after you use each cheque, which means that you do not make a large hole in your cheque account before leaving for your holiday. While abroad, you write Eurocheques in the local currency and if you need more than the equivalent of £100 simply write out as many cheques as you need, present them together with your Eurocheque card, and the hotel, bank or retailer writes the card number on the back of each cheque to guarantee it. In most countries local banks make no charge whatsoever when you cash a Eurocheque so that if, for example, you write a cheque for 500 francs, you receive exactly 500 francs.

However, when the cheque is received by your own bank for payment, a small commission is paid to the foreign bank and a minimal handling fee for each cheque is charged on top of the normal bank charges you pay at home. There is also a nominal charge for the card itself.

FOREIGN CURRENCY

Whichever country you are visiting, you are likely to need some foreign currency for paying taxi fares and the odd meal or drink before you reach your final destination. Do not forget also that if you arrive at the weekend, some local banks may not be open until the next Monday morning. Some countries have a limit on the amount of foreign currency you are allowed to take in and out of the country. Also, some large denomination notes can be difficult to exchange when you return to this country and banks will not change any foreign coins. If you plan carefully you should be able to get rid of any small change before the end of your stay, but if not, pass it on to the Handicapped Aid Trust (see page 8).

BANKING HOURS ABROAD

As previously mentioned, banking hours abroad may vary from those in this country. Generally speaking, banks are open Monday to Friday, (although in most Moslem countries they will be closed Friday and open on Sunday instead). Opening hours vary considerably though they will usually open in the morning in most countries. In Southern Europe, however, they may then close for around three hours before re-opening in the late afternoon. Check banking hours with your hotel manager or the local tourist information centre and do not forget that national holidays and religious festivals are likely to mean that the banks are closed.

If you are desperate for cash, most large hotels will usually cash your Travellers' cheques but you may find yourself getting an unfavourable rate of exchange. The answer is to plan ahead so that you will have sufficient cash to last from day to day.

SECURITY

Always carry your passport, money, Eurocheques, Eurocheque Card, Travellers' cheques and credit cards in a safe place and never leave them, for example, in your hotel room or car. Always keep a record of your Travellers' cheque and Eurocheque transactions and keep your Eurocheques and Eurocheque card separate. Never sign Eurocheques or Travellers' cheques except in the presence of the person cashing your cheque and always provide some proof of identity (ideally your passport) when cashing your Travellers' cheques.

Some hotels will be happy to look after your passport and other valuables in the hotel safe and for absolute security this may be a good idea.

If you follow these simple rules and always make sure you have access to extra money for emergencies, you should not hit any problems. However, should you lose your Travellers' cheques, Eurocheques or Eurocheque card then you must notify your account holding branch immediately, as well as the local police.

Finally, it is a good idea to have some pounds and pence on you so that you can buy a meal or something to read if you get held up at the airport or before boarding ship. Keep some spare cash available for the journey home as well.

CHAPTER FOUR

MEDICAL MATTERS

IMMUNISATION

If you are visiting a hot country you may wish to find out more about health precautions and whether vaccination or inoculation against infectious or contagious diseases is recommended.

Before You Go, leaflet SA 40 available from your travel agent or DoH Leaflets Unit, should provide you with all the information you need to know about vaccination requirements. MASTA (The Medical Advisory Service to Travellers Abroad), a service run by the London School of Tropical Medicine, can give advice to those people travelling to exotic destinations and can also tell you all about immunisation and other procedures to ensure a healthy holiday. It hopes to start a 'Phone Home' scheme which will give details about local hospital facilities, addresses of English-speaking doctors, lists of drugs and their names in the country you are visiting, etc. It also issues a free leaflet on Acquired Immune Deficiency Syndrome (AIDS).

British Airways offers an immunisation service at its London Regent Street office (Tel: 071-439 9584) and at Heathrow Airport (Tel: 081-562 5825). Some useful items for intrepid travellers (such as mosquito netting!) can be found at BA's Regent Street travel shop. For up-to-date information about vaccination requirements, contact the Department of Health or Thomas Cook's London office. The National Tourist Office of the country you intend to visit can also advise you about immunisation and health regulations. Your doctor can tell you where to go for specialist advice. Leaflet SA 41 *While You're Away* includes an application form to obtain Document E111 for medical treatment abroad.

However, it is recommended that you take out a fully comprehensive insurance if you are a disabled traveller (see Chapter 2, *Doing The Paperwork*).

If you are travelling to a country which requires vaccination against infectious diseases, you will need to make an appointment to have this done several months before you travel and, in some cases, you must allow adequate intervals between vaccination doses. If you travel before a complete vaccination course has been given you may not be fully immunised. Visitors to European countries or Mediterranean resorts do not usually require vaccination. Vaccinations are given for Yellow fever, Polio, Typhoid, Hepatitis A, Cholera, Tetanus and Malaria.

SOME SIMPLE PRECAUTIONS FOR A HEALTHY HOLIDAY

Food

It has been said that 'travel broadens the mind and loosens the bowels' and bearing this in mind, whatever foreign country you are visiting (but particularly the tropics, the Middle East and some Mediterranean resorts), you should take precautions against 'holiday tummy' which could completely spoil your trip. Diarrhoea hits 40 per cent of all travellers, and for disabled travellers it is not just a nuisance. It can be the sort of disaster which could put you off travelling ever again, so it is extremely important to prevent it if possible. This can best be achieved through careful attention to food hygiene. Avoid salad, raw shellfish, and peeled fruit, unless you know it has been thoroughly washed, and unpasteurised milk and cream. If you are worried about eating food at a particular place, choose food that has been freshly cooked and fruit that can be easily peeled like bananas, citrus fruits or melon. If you think that the plates and cutlery look a bit dubious, you could resort to rinsing them in a drop of hot tea, or a small amount of alcohol. Cutlery can also be cleaned up with an alcohol-soaked injection swab or flamed with a candle or lighter if you have the facilities for this kind of operation. If a cup looks a bit grubby, pour away a little of a hot drink to rinse the rim.

Drinking the water

If you are unsure about drinking the water, you could take chlorine tablets with you to sterilise it or, alternatively, use reputable makes of bottled water for drinking and for cleaning your teeth. However hot you may be, avoid ice cubes in drinks; they are likely to consist of local water. It may be a good idea to travel with one of those widely available travel jugs with dual voltage, or a cup immersion heater (known as a Hot Rod) so that you can boil up your water and then leave it to cool in sterile containers. A travel jug also comes in handy for making a 'cuppa' when you are longing for a decent cup of tea. Boiling your drinking water is a simple but reliable method of sterilisation. One drop of tincture of iodine will purify a cup of water or drink, or paper cartridge filters will filter out impurities in the water.

First Aid Kit

Below are some items that you may want to include in your 'Travellers' First Aid Kit'. You may want to double up on some items and leave out others according to your own personal needs and the facilities at your destination.

Some precautionary items might include:

- Water purifying tables, such as 'Puritabs'
- Preparations to cope with diarrhoea (available without prescription from your chemist). Imodium capsules are said to be very good, as is Codein Phosphate, or Lomotil. The two latter drugs require prescription. If you are struck down with diarrhoea the most important thing to do is to replace the lost fluid. Keep off alcohol and starve yourself for 24 hours. Oral rehydration solutions are an effective method of replacing lost fluids and salts. You can buy sachets of rehydration salts from your chemist containing all the essential salts and minerals you will need, or you can make your own rehydration mixture from four heaped teaspoons of sugar or honey and a half-teaspoon of salt added to one litre of clean water
- Insect repellent for mosquito and gnat bites. Oil of citronella can be rubbed on all exposed skin to ward off insect bites and it smells pleasant. If a strong insect repellent is recommended (for people who react badly to bites), use one containing diethyl toluamide

  'Jungle Formula' is excellent, and others include 'Auten', 'Sketofax' or 'Dusk Insect Repellent'. All come in aerosols or lotions, and are available from your local chemist
- Antiseptic medication (for treating mosquito or gnat bites) such as tetracycline ointment or gentamycin cream, should always be carried and applied to any bite immediately
- If you are prone to urinary tract infections, remember to pack an antibiotic such as Septrin, just in case!
- Tanning preparations which contain a screening factor
- Sunburn soothing lotion, calamine lotion
- Plant spray for cooling down (good artificial sweat for tetras!)
- Paracetamol for headaches
- Bisodol for indigestion.

Insect Bites

Insect bites can be very painful and cause varying degrees of discomfort. Insects can also spread serious diseases and protection against them should be given top priority, especially if you are camping. If you are travelling to a country which is plagued by insects you should take every precaution to protect yourself from bites.

Usually, mosquitoes are more of a nuisance than a hazard on holiday but a large number of diseases are insect borne and in some people bites can swell up and become infected. There is no point in ruining your holiday for the sake of an aerosol or insect repellent and we have included some brand names which have a good reputation and which are available from your local chemist, so track them down before departing for warmer climes. Aerosols are good for clearing out mosquitoes that are lurking in your bedroom last thing at night! Also, if you keep your windows open at night insects are attracted by any lights you leave on and when sipping drinks at that romantic waterside bar after dusk, remember to keep all exposed parts of the skin covered, either with fabric or insect repellent.

- While in a wheelchair you could try soaking cotton shoes and socks with a solution of citronella or use an anklet soaked in insect repellent to ward off bites on the feet and ankles
- Anti-histamines will help to damp down prickly heat rash or itching caused by insect bites. Some anti-histamines make people feel sleepy, but Terfanadine (Teldane, Tricludan) or Astemizole (Hismanal) tablets do not
- Anti-fungal dusting powder to keep you cool is useful if you are visiting a humid area, or travelling on a plane
- Some dry dressings such as Melolin in case of cuts, bruises or sores. If you do need them while abroad, they may be difficult to obtain
- Alcohol-soaked wipes in small sachets for cleaning minor wounds (at a pinch they can also be used on suspicious-looking plates and cutlery when eating out!)
- A thermometer
- Toilet paper - many public loos abroad do not always supply it!

Most drugs have two names, a generic, or scientific name which is usually the same or similar in most countries, and a trade or brand name which may vary from country to country. You should always carry a spare prescription of your medication giving its generic name in case further supplies are needed in an emergency.

Too much sun...

Travellers who are not used to the sun or who are visiting very hot countries where the temperatures soar should beware. Heat stroke can be a killer!

It might be worth investing in a small battery-operated fan before you go if you know you will be sitting around in very hot temperatures, although these can usually be found at sunny resorts. Keep your plant spray at the ready and do not forget your sun hat.

Water intake requirements in a hot country are very high. Keep topping up with long cool drinks (devoid of alcohol) to keep your urine pale in colour. Dark, concentrated urine is a sign of dehydration. If you do become dehydrated and have not bought any rehydration salts along with you, it is possible to make a solution from local products. You will need four heaped teaspoons of sugar or honey and a half-teaspoon of salt, added to one litre of clean (sterile) water.

If you insist on a tan, and most of us want to come home with at least some indication that we have returned from Marbella and not Mablethorpe, then take it very easy. Ideally you should start by exposing your skin for only 20 minutes a day for the first day or two. Use a highly protective sun barrier cream, replacing it every hour or so, and particularly after swimming. Over the next few days gradually increase your exposure and use a lower factor sunscreen to let in a few more ultra-violet rays. Skin types usually fall into one of five categories:

- very sensitive skin which always burns and never tans
- sensitive skin which tans slowly and burns easily
- fair skin which tans gradually and burns easily
- normal skin which tans easily sometimes burns
- dark skin which tans easily and smoothly and rarely burns.

Once you have identified your skin type, you can work out which Sun Protection Factor (SPF) you need. If the natural protection time of your skin, ie the amount of time you can stay exposed to sun without burning, is 10 minutes then theoretically, wearing a sun protection factor of 12 means you can stay in the sun 12 times longer before you burn. (10 x 12 = 120 minutes). The more sensitive the skin, the higher the SPF should be. If you start with the strongest you can the move down the scale, according to your skin type.

If you have very sensitive skin you may decide to use a total sun block on the body's danger spots - lips, nose, neck, ears, shoulders, knees, ankles and feet, or on paralysed limbs that only see the light of day two weeks of the year.

Always moisturise with an after sun cream or baby lotion last thing at night to reduce skin dryness.

Some people make the mistake of over-doing it during the first few days and suffer the consequences - painful burning, swelling, blistering and peeling. Never sit in the sun without the protection of clothes and/or a barrier cream. Remember that the shade of a palm tree does not necessarily protect you from the sun's rays reflected from nearby sea or sand; you can get burnt splashing around in the swimming pool!

Today's efficient sun barrier preparations - creams, gels or lotions, should allow you to arrive home with a golden tan.

The effects of too much sun for tetraplegics whose sweating ability is often seriously impaired, can cause heat stroke (sunstroke), whereby sweating diminishes and the body temperature rises. So, if your sweating mechanism isn't working properly, it is particularly important to take adequate precautions. The warning signs are a dull pounding headache and a general feeling of strangeness. If you develop these symptoms and too much sun is suspected, act immediately. Sit in the shade, remove as much clothing as possible, cover your body with a wet towel or sheet and start spraying with water and fanning to promote cooling by evaporation.

If you do get sunburnt use calamine cream or lotion to soothe burnt areas, and a mild analgesic such as aspirin or paracetamol to relieve pain and inflamation. Severe sunburn can be treated by keeping the area clean to avoid infection, drinking plenty of fluids, and bed rest. Do not sunbathe the day after any bad burn but allow healing to take place for a few days. Always seek the advice of a doctor if the condition deteriorates.

Alcohol

Do not be tempted to overdo the alcohol just because you are on holiday! Cheap drinks and relaxation can combine to spoil

your trip. And do not forget that alcohol is a drug which can cause dehydration without any help from the sun! Put the two together and you could have a problem. The message is quite simple - drink in moderation, keep up a high non-alcoholic fluid intake and if possible save the alcohol for the cooler evenings.

Finally, an indispensable guide is ***Traveller's Health*** by Richard Dawood (Oxford University Press). This gives advice on all aspects of health abroad, from what to do if you develop a raging toothache while soaking up the sun in Tenerife, to coping with lassa fever.

Accessible wheelchair loos are, of course, fairly elusive, whichever country you are travelling in. If you are sticking to the main autoroutes or motorways, accessible toilets will be found at petrol service stations, but if you intend to meander down 'B' roads, the likelihood is that you will not find a convenient convenience. The best idea is to head towards the larger towns and drive to the railway or coach station where there will be toilet facilities, often with adapted loos. On the whole, public toilets may not be as spotlessly clean as one would like.

INCONTINENCE AIDS AND IDEAS

For men, the situation is not so dire, as they can pull in to a convenient lay-by and empty their leg bag or use a urinal, which can also be fitted with a non-spill adaptor to prevent leakage if there is no convenient place to empty it straight away. Also available is a disposable plastic collector which has a built-in non-returnable valve. These pack flat and are sold in boxes of 10 and are an ideal solution to male incontinence on holiday or travelling in a car.

For women the solution is not so easy. Some women SIA members use female urinals with great success, others find it completely impossible to manoeuvre themselves in to the correct position. Female urinals are much smaller and more portable than hospital-type bedpans, and so if you can master the technique they are ideal items to include in your packing or place discreetly under the seat of your car.

There are several types suitable for disabled women, and ideally you should go to your local aids centre where you can judge their usefulness for yourself. The fracture bedpan is wedge-shaped and designed to be slipped under the body without raising the pelvis. Two smaller female urinals are the 'St Peters Boat' which is a pointed dish with a handle which can be slipped easily between the legs while sitting or the 'Slipper' type which is a small shallow dish with an inward curving splash proof rim and a capped hollow handle through which it can be emptied. The edges of this one are nicely rounded so as not to create any unwanted pressure. This dish can be slipped under the buttocks without having to raise the hips, and is small enough to manage with one hand. The swan-type female urinal is similar to a male urinal, but with a wider neck which is specially shaped to be held close to the body. If you are more agile, there are now several female urinals available specifically designed for use in a car or in limited space. These urinals consist of a moulded plastic section, contoured to fit the female body, with a short handle in front by means of which it can be held comfortably and firmly in position.

A disposable plastic bag with an elasticated top fits over the rim of the device and is suspended from it to collect the urine. It can be used while sitting. The bag can be emptied, disposed of or if necessary re-used. The urinal is small and light and can be carried in a handbag. Or you could try a do-it-yourself device made from a soft plastic funnel (available from the wine-making counter of Boots the chemist). Connect the funnel to a length of plastic tubing and use a hot water bottle as a collecting bag. Alternatively, the tube could lead out of the car directly into the gutter. Details of where to obtain the above aids are obtainable from SIA or the Disabled Living Foundation. Whatever method you use, it is always best to practise before you go away to familiarise yourself with it.

An 'Easinurse cushion' has openings or removable sections to accommodate a bedpan or other receptacle and can be positioned on your wheelchair or car seat. However, not everyone finds it easy to sit in the correct position.

It is well worth considering a collapsible transportable commode, which is light and easy to fold and which will take up little room in the car. It may be the most important item you pack, as it is possible to use a commode in a quiet lay-by with the help of the car door and some temporary screening for a little privacy. A portable commode can also come in handy to use over low toilets when stopping at overnight accommodation, and will provide a set of instant grab rails if you need them.

Some disabled people use a Carter's folding commode with detachable arms and swinging detachable footrests and recommend one with brakes on all four castors for stability. Your local Aids Centre can supply commodes on castors on loan as they count as wheelchairs, but you might have to do some persuasive negotiating to get the model you want. These types of commodes can also double as a bidet and wheelchair in very confined spaces like a caravan, cottage or foreign hotel bathroom.

Suppliers of incontinence aids

Always try your local Disabled Living Centre or District or Home Nursing Service who may be able to help and advise with the provision of incontinence aids and equipment. The Disabled Living Foundation can provide a list of suppliers.

- **William Freeman & Co Ltd**
  Suba-Seal Works, Wakefield Road
  Staincross, Barnsley
  S.Yorkshire S75 6DH
  Tel: (0226) 284081
  (Female urinal 'Slipper' dish)

- **Thakeray Care**
  Great George Street
  Leeds LS1 3BB
  Tel: (0532) 430028
  (Non-spill adaptor for male urinals and other incontinence aids).

- **Incare Medical Products**
  43 Castle Street, Reading
  Berkshire RG1 7SN
  Tel: (0734) 597211

- **Leyland Medical Ltd (Peoplecare)**
  15 Colvestone Crescent, Dalston
  London E8 2LN
  Tel: 071-254 6571

- **Smith and Nephew Medical Ltd**
  P O Box 81, Hessle Road
  Hull HU3 2BN
  Tel: (0482) 5181

MEDICAL DIRECTORY

Useful addresses

- **British Airways**
  Immunisation Service and Travel Shop/Clinic
  156 Regent Street, London W1
  Tel: 071-439 9584/5

- **Thomas Cook Ltd**
  45 Berkeley Street
  London W1
  Tel: 071-499 4000

- **Department of Health**
  International Branch
  Hannibal House,
  Elephant & Castle
  London SE1 6TE
  Tel: 071-972 2000 ext 6749

- **Vaccination Centre**
  Hospital for Tropical Diseases
  4 St Pancras Way
  London NW1 OPE
  Tel: 071-388 9600/071-388 8989

- **The London School of Hygiene and Tropical Medicine**
  Kepple Street
  London WC1E 7HT
  Tel: 071-636 7921

- **MASTA**
  (Medical Advisory Service to Travellers Abroad)
  Tel: 071-631 4408

CHAPTER FIVE

LUGGAGE, PACKING AND CUSTOMS

Once you have made your travel arrangements, booked your hotel, checked that your passport is in order and either had any necessary 'jabs' or made an appointment for them to be done, you can turn your attention to the packing.

When it comes to this important task, people generally seem to fall into two categories; those who begin packing when their holiday is still two weeks off, and those who leave it until the night before - and live to regret it. It is best to place yourself somewhere in the middle of these two extremes. After all, if you pack too early you may find yourself constantly unpacking to get at that blouse/shirt/hairbrush you need, and if you pack too late you could end up throwing in everything but the kitchen sink in your panic to get done, and find yourself having to pay excess luggage charges! Far better, as with the rest of your holiday, to plan early and think ahead.

CHOOSING YOUR LUGGAGE

Most manufacturers are now producing ultra-lightweight luggage which is both attractive and easy to handle. This type of luggage is not necessarily expensive - look in your high street chain store for good,

strong, well-designed cases. Choose distinctive looking luggage (brightly coloured or with a bold stripe) and you will easily be able to spot your case at the baggage collection point or, for that matter, describe it should it go astray. The soft top, zip around variety is probably easiest to handle, and tetraplegics can fix key rings to the zip fasteners to make them easier to open and shut. Opt for one-handled bags; those with two handles will suffer from being thrown around by baggage handlers. Small wheels on cases make them easier to pull along, so choose a case that has these already fitted, or buy a set which can be easily fixed round the case by means of elastic straps. When choosing your luggage remember that to fit under a plane seat, a case must not be over 18 x 14 x 6 inches. Pick one with at least one accessible outside pocket in which to keep passport and other travel documents (and keep the pocket turned in towards you for security). A shoulder strap is also useful if you are carrying your own hand luggage and many find a lightweight nylon holdall very useful as you can squash lots into it, and either carry it on your lap or hooked over your wheelchair handles, leaving your hands free. Put your name, address and telephone number on a label inside the lid of your main case so that, should the outer label be lost, your luggage can still be traced for you. Instead of using tie-on labels with your name and address for the outside of your case, use stick-on labels. That way they cannot be removed and you will not find yourself returning home to a house that has been burgled in your absence!

Finally, do remember not to pack valuables in your case and, most important, to lock your luggage.

Packing

If you travel often, you probably have packing down to a fine art, realising the benefits of travelling light and keeping luggage to a minimum. Before you start to pack, make a list of what you think you should take. Then rip it up and make another list, this time cutting it down to things you ***really*** need (one good tip is to halve the amount of clothes you think you will need and double your money!) If you are going to a hot country, take light, cool, loose clothing and do remember that even in hot climates, evening temperatures can drop rapidly; so add a warm jumper or wrap to slip on in the evening. During the day, however, do not forget a hat to keep you cool while the temperature climbs.

ESSENTIAL ITEMS

Those travelling to a colder climate must pack plenty of thin but warm clothes to enable dressing in layers - this keeps you warmer than one piece of heavy clothing as heat is trapped between layers. And do not forget the thermal underwear!

If you are planning lots of sightseeing, make sure you add extra pushing gloves to your list as you will be surprised at the rate they wear out.

Make sure you have enough condoms, bungs, tubes, drainage bags, pads, medicine (if you take it), etc., on your list. You may not easily be able to get what you need if you are going abroad so take enough and perhaps a little more to cover yourself for emergencies. All these items are classified as 'medical supplies' and are carried free (more on that later).

Have you put a plant spray on your list? If you are tetraplegic and have difficulty sweating, you can create artificial perspiration by spraying your face, neck and shoulders liberally with cold water from a plant spray. People may wonder what you are doing, but it is less messy than swooning nose down into the spaghetti carbonara as the temperature soars.

Once you start packing tick off each item as it goes into the case and keep your list handy for double checking. If you have chosen crease-resistant materials you need not wrap clothes in tissue paper to avoid wrinkles. Pack shoes down the side of your case and in plastic bags (bin liners will do) to avoid damaging your clothes. Avoid packing anything in glass bottles - they will break and cause a horrible mess. Instead use plastic bottles, leave a gap between the top of the contents and the cap, and secure the cap with sticky tape. Take more sticky tape for the return journey. Rather than taking aerosols if you are flying- they have been known to explode because of reduced pressure - take atomisers which are quite easily available nowadays in this ozone layer-conscious world.

As most hotels provide adequate clothes hangers you need not use up your precious space by packing them. Instead you could take one of the new lightweight travelling irons with suitable adaptor (although some hotels will lend you an iron on request). This will be particularly useful if you are on a business trip and you want to arrive for your meeting looking well-groomed. If you do not have an iron try hanging creased clothes in a steamy bathroom.

Naturally you will pack in your hand luggage anything you may need *en route*, so remember to pack in your main luggage only those items you will not need until you have arrived at your destination.

Emergency Items

It is a good idea to pack some 'emergency' items for possible use on the flight in your hand luggage and add extra medication for the holiday:

- spare catheters
- leg bags
- bungs
- glue
- condoms
- a plastic screw top container for leg bag emptying
- leather strap or wheelchair narrower
- plastic covering for the aircraft seat (in case you are worried about leaking)
- wheelchair repair outfit
- woolly for temperature drops.

Stow your bag under the seat in front of you (not in the overhead locker, where you will not be able to get at it). It can be useful if you have much luggage to make a note, even just a mental one, of what is in which case. This will avoid the cry of 'where have I put my glasses/raincoat/Travel Scrabble?'

If you are going away with a friend or other members of your family, share your clothing between cases - that way if one case goes astray you will not be left in only the clothes you 'stand up' (or perhaps 'sit down') in!

Finally, as most people seem to return with more possessions than they left with, leave enough space in your suitcase for souvenirs and mementoes of your trip.

Customs

When you enter a foreign country, and on your return to the United Kingdom, you will pass through Customs and must declare any items you have in excess of the duty and tax free allowances. There are also a number of prohibited or restricted goods which you are not allowed to bring into the United Kingdom, ranging from the fairly obvious (controlled drugs, firearms, counterfeit currency), to the faintly bizarre (tree bark and stuffed birds).

As the duty free allowances change depending on the generosity of the Chancellor of the Exchequer in his annual Budget, they are not listed here. However, they are clearly displayed at airports and Channel ports. In addition, you can obtain a copy of Customs Notice 1 from your local Customs and Excise Office (address and telephone number in local telephone directory) or from:

HM Customs & Excise
New Kings Beam House
Upper Ground
London SE1 9PJ
Tel: 071-620 1313

When you arrive at Customs, you should go through the Green Channel if you have nothing to declare, ie you have not exceeded your duty free allowance, or through the Red Channel if you have.

To save time and to avoid confusion it may be useful to make a list of everything you have to declare such as purchases in excess of the duty and tax-free allowances. Carry receipts for any valuable items such as cameras, radios and watches that were bought retail in the United Kingdom or have been brought through United Kingdom Customs before and had duty and/or tax paid on them. If you are in any doubt, go through the Red Channel and the Customs Officer will advise you.

Whichever channel you go through, the Customs Officer is legally entitled to examine your luggage (you are responsible for opening, unpacking and repacking your luggage).

Do not be tempted to hide anything or attempt to mislead the Customs officers - it is not worth it. The penalties are high (as is the humiliation!) And do not think the extra bottle of Scotch stuffed inside a wheelchair cushion will escape notice - it is the first place they will look, and you might get a pressure sore into the bargain!

If you do have to pay duty and/or value added tax (VAT), you will normally have to do so before leaving the baggage hall. You should keep receipts given in case you bring the same goods through United Kingdom Customs again.

DRUGS

If you need to take prescribed medicines abroad with you it is your responsibility to know what you can take in and out of the UK and other countries. The Embassy or representatives of the country you are going to visit will advise you on that country's drug laws and the Home Office Drugs Branch (Tel: 071-273 3806) will tell you about the UK regulations. Carry a letter from your doctor giving details of the drugs presc ed. Remember that some medicines which are available over the counter in the UK may be subject to control in other countries.

CHAPTER SIX

TRAVELLING BY AIR

Travelling by air is, of course, usually the quickest way to reach your destination abroad. Some disabled people, particularly those newly injured, may be unsure of the procedures to ensure a trouble-free flight and may, in fact, be put off flying by the thought of a long journey in which getting to the lavatory appears to be a problem. However, these days airlines are greatly improving their facilities for disabled people so that travelling with a disability need not present such a problem any more. For disabled passengers there are still some hurdles to overcome, and a spirit of adventure is definitely an advantage. Some airlines are better than others, both as regards facilities on board and in their attitude towards disabled travellers, so it is a good idea to shop around before finally booking your ticket.

Most modern airport buildings have been designed to accommodate the needs of people with disabilities and all the major UK airports have leaflets explaining the facilities they offer to disabled travellers. This includes the location of ramps, lifts, wide-door wheelchair accessible toilets, telephones for wheelchair-users, and car parking facilities for disabled people.

MEDICAL CLEARANCE

At the time of booking your flight, you should inform the travel agent or airline of the kind of assistance you will need at the airport and for getting on and off the aircraft. The responsibility for helping you will be shared between the airport management, the airline you are travelling with and its handling agents, so make sure they are all aware of your requirements.

The day before departure, check direct with the airline reservation desk, the special facilities desk who take care of disabled passengers, or the customer services department of the airline you are flying with, to make sure all your special needs have been fully understood. Also make sure that the airport at your destination, or any stopover *en route* where you intend disembarking, is fully aware of your disability and any special service you will need.

It is debatable whether it should be necessary for disabled travellers with a static, non-progressive disability to have to fill in forms before they are allowed to enjoy the same advantages as their able-bodied companions and some disabled travellers feel strongly that it should be resisted. However, the most important thing the airline wants to know is whether you can take care of your own needs on board the plane without the help of cabin staff. It will want to know what arrangements you have made if you cannot get to or use the aircraft toilet unassisted; for example, whether you have an indwelling catheter, a urinary collection device, extra padding and protective pants, or are simply restricting your fluids. It will then decide whether the method you are using is acceptable to the airline. This is because cabin staff are classified as 'food handlers' and as such are not allowed to give disabled travellers any personal help in the toilet or while sitting on the aircraft seat (e.g. emptying leg bags etc). If you are unable to look after your own toilet requirements on the flight, the airline may insist on your travelling with a companion.

INCAD FORM

Incapacitated Passengers Handling Advice - INCAD has now replaced the Standard Medical Information Form - MEDIF and travellers using wheelchairs will probably be required to complete one of these. Most airlines using long haul scheduled routes will ask for an INCAD form to be filled in and sent to them prior to travel. However, most carriers operating charter flights to holiday destinations will not bother with this, but will, of course, want to know about your disability and what assistance you require.

Part 1 of the INCAD form covers handling advice which is filled in by your travel agent or whoever makes the booking from information supplied by you. It must state the kind of individual help needed at the airport, in getting on and off the plane, during the flight and in an emergency evacuation. Arrangements will then be made to assist you throughout your journey.

Part 2 covers medical clearance, and is usually required only for passengers who have an illness or disease or who are recovering from an operation. If it applies to you, it should be completed by your doctor. However, sometimes it is easier for all concerned if you fill in the relevant details and ask your doctor to OK and sign it. Airline cabin staff are trained to deal with in-flight emergencies, but do not carry out any routine or preplanned nursing or medical care.

FREMEC CARD

If, after your first trip abroad, you have enjoyed yourself so much that you decide you want to repeat the experience, then a FREMEC card (Frequent Travellers Medical Card) is a 'must' for anyone travelling often by air. The FREMEC card is issued free to disabled passengers who travel regularly and who, in the opinion of the airlines' medical officer, have a stable medical condition. Possession of a FREMEC card will avoid the need to obtain medical clearance and an INCAD Form every time you fly as it describes your disability and special requirements when travelling. To obtain one of these useful cards, apply to the airline you intend travelling with. The FREMEC card is accepted by most major airlines who are members of the IATA (International Air Transport Association). However, possession of a FREMEC card does not eliminate the need for prior notification of your disability and flight requirements.

GETTING TO THE AIRPORT

By Car or Taxi

The most convenient way of travelling to the airport is usually by car. However, as car parking arrangements vary from airport to airport, it is always best to find out what facilities are offered to disabled people before embarking on your journey. Generally, if you display an orange badge on a private car the driver will be able to stop briefly to set you down. If you want your driver to accompany you to the check-in desk, it is advisable to explain where you are going to a policeman or traffic warden before leaving the car unattended.

Parking Your Car

If you are driving your own car to the airport and want to leave it there while you are on holiday, most airports have long-term car parks.

Some airports will offer a special service to take you from the long-term car park to the terminal, but it is essential that you arrange this in advance with the airport authorities.

Heathrow International Airport

Heathrow is the world's premier international airport and London's largest, with four passenger terminals. At Heathrow there are disabled car parking bays provided at each of the short term car parks, except 1A, which is located close to entrances and lifts. Long term car parks have a special minibus service for disabled drivers which is available on request. On arriving at the long term car park report to the reception and inform the car park official that you require this service. You will be directed to a car parking bay reserved for disabled drivers and a wheelchair accessible minibus will take you to the passenger terminal building. On your return, use the telephone at the long term bus stop outside the terminal building to ask for the wheelchair accessible minibus to take you to your car.

A list of up-to-date charges for both short and long term parking, together with other useful information, is available in the guide to Heathrow Airport entitled ***Take Off***. Contact the Publications Department, Heathrow Airport Ltd, D'Albiac House, Heathrow Airport, Hounslow, Middlesex TW6 1JH for a copy.

Airbus Service

London Transport operates frequent Airbus services linking Heathrow's four terminals with various points in Central London. Buses operating on Airbus services are adapted to carry two passengers in wheelchairs. Airbus A1 connects Victoria with Central London Carelink service, which uses smaller buses equipped with wheelchair lifts and serves Paddington, Euston, King's Cross, Liverpool Street and Waterloo stations. For further details of Carelink, telephone 071-222 1234.

Gatwick International Airport

Gatwick is the second busiest international airport in the world, handling over 19 million passengers a year. It now has two terminals, the North - the most recently built and the most modern - and the South terminal. Both have parking facilities for orange badge holders in both the short and long term car parks, but there are no concessions for disabled people and normal charges apply. Short term parking can be found at the North terminal, where reserved bays for vehicles displaying the orange badge can be found on level one of each short-term multi-storey car park. Access to the terminal is by ramps and bridges.

Long term parking

For long-term parking at either terminal, telephone in advance indicating the extent of your disability and arrangements will be made to take you to the North or South terminal buildings. For the North terminal phone Euro Car Parks on Gatwick (0293) 502747 and for the South terminal phone NCP on Gatwick (0293) 502896.

Current parking charges together with other useful information about the services offered to people with disabilities, can be found in ***Passenger Information*** a booklet available from the Public Relations Department, Gatwick Airport Ltd, Gatwick, West Sussex.

Luton International Airport

At Luton Airport open-air car parking is available and disabled drivers are advised to write in advance to the Airport Director to ensure a parking place adjacent to the Terminal Building. Normal charges will apply. Contact the Car Park Manager on (0582) 405100 ext. 270. For information about undercover car parking telephone Luton (0582) 261189. Current car parking charges and other facilities for the wheelchair traveller can be found in the booklet ***Passenger Information*** available from the Marketing Department, Luton International Airport, Luton, Bedfordshire LU2 9LY.

Stansted Airport

At Stansted there are parking spaces available for orange badge holders within about 100 yards of the terminal. It is advisable to telephone the British Airports duty officer on (0279) 502387 before you travel, so that arrangements can be made to get you to the terminal building from the car park. A leaflet containing some information on facilities for disabled travellers is available from the Marketing Department, Stansted Airport, Stansted, Essex CM24 8QW. Tel: (0279) 502380.

Manchester Airport

Manchester Airport (Ringway) is just under 10 miles south of Manchester city centre and is well signposted from the M56 and central Manchester. There is a drop-off point for passengers on level 5 of the short-term car park at the entrance to the check-in hall and a pick-up point by the arrivals hall.

If you need assistance from your car to the check-in desk help is available from Door No. 2. There is a vehicle capable of lifting wheelchairs up to the door level of the plane and the terminal building is fully accessible for disabled travellers. If you wish to use these special facilities ring 061-489 3817 with your flight number and time of departure the day before you travel and arrangements will be made to assist you.

Newcastle Airport

Newcastle is a small, friendly airport situated at Woolsington, 6 miles from the city and reached via the Central Motorway East and the A696. There is a short-term car park opposite the terminal building. The long-term car park is to the left of the entrance to the terminal building. All facilities in the terminal building are fully accessible to wheelchair passengers. You are advised to contact the airline you are flying with to make any special arrangements. Access to the plane is by mini-bus with a tail lift to the aircraft door, so disabled passengers do not have to use steps. Further help from the Information Desk. Tel: 091-286 0966.

Birmingham Airport

Responsibility for the needs of disabled travellers at this airport is shared between the airline concerned and the Airport Authority Company. When making a reservation always tell the airport, or your travel agent, that you are a wheelchair user so that they can make arrangements to help you at the airport or during the flight.

Facilities at the Terminal Building include wheelchair-accessible toilets, and public telephones at a suitable height. An Information Desk is sited on the main ground floor concourse and all passenger facilities are easily accessible on the ground and first floors by using the signposted lifts and escalators.

If you are planning to leave your car at the airport, you will find that 12 spaces are reserved for disabled people in long stay car park I and eight spaces on the ground floor of the multi-storey car park adjacent to the terminal building and reached by a covered walkway. Should you require any assistance, press the 'assist button' situated at the barrier to the entrance/exit of the car park. There are adapted loos in the multi-storey car park (the keys are held in the car park control room).

For passenger embarkation/disembarkation you can either stay in your own wheelchair or use the purpose-built lift vehicle. In either event, airlines make their own arrangements for disabled travellers and will happily offer assistance.

Feedback from disabled people who have used Birmingham International Airport shows a high degree of satisfaction with the facilities provided. This may be because the Managing Director of the airport is himself a wheelchair user and knows exactly what disabled people need!

If you are travelling to or from Glasgow, Edinburgh, Prestwick or Aberdeen, a booklet called ***Scottish Airports Information***, available from Scottish Airports Ltd, St Andrews Drive, Glasgow Airport, Paisley PA3 2SW, telephone 041-887 1111, gives some information for disabled passengers together with telephone numbers for the Information Desk and Airport Duty Manager of each airport.

For those who decide on an overnight stay near the airport, there are many wheelchair accessible hotels in the vicinity. Some of these hotels will allow their overnight guests to leave their car on the hotel premises and drive them to the airport in a hotel-owned vehicle. A charge is made for this service.

Further information about wheelchair-accessible hotels can be found in the information booklets published by the individual airports, some of which use the wheelchair symbol and ***Holidays in the British Isles***, published by RADAR.

It may be worthwhile contacting commercial firms around the major airports who organise parking, pick-up and set-down services to and from the airport. This may be cheaper than using the long term car park at the airport for several weeks. Some of the parking service firms can transport disabled people to the airport in a saloon car, so if you are able to transfer comfortably into the front seat of a car this may be an alternative option.

Voluntary Organisations

Transport to and from the airport could also be arranged through a local voluntary agency such as the British Red Cross Society, WRVS, or the Social Services Department. Dial-a-Ride or Community Transport schemes will help if you live within their catchment area, and even if you do not it might be worth a phone call to find out if they can offer any assistance, or know someone who can. Triscope is a nationwide travel and transport advice service designed specifically to help disabled and elderly people plan their journeys. Tel: 081-994 9294.

By Train

British Rail runs a service from Victoria Station to Gatwick Airport, called the Gatwick Express. The service is fully accessible to people in wheelchairs and no advance notice to travel is necessary. For some Gatwick flights it is possible to check in and hand over your luggage at Victoria Railway Station Air Terminal, so that on arrival at the airport you can go straight through Passport Control to the final departure lounge.

Whether you are travelling by car, coach or train - the golden rule is - leave plenty of time!

BAGGAGE

If you cannot use the baggage trolleys provided for passengers and there is not a porter available when you arrive, contact a uniformed member of the airport staff, or go straight to the information desk for help.

CHECKING-IN

Most airlines prefer that disabled travellers arrive an hour-and-a-half (or more) earlier than other passengers. Despite prior notification, there may be some delay in organising a porter or handling staff to bring the airport wheelchair or electric buggy for transfer to the plane. At Terminal 4 building at London's Heathrow Airport passengers using wheelchairs can find a special check-in (Desk 63) which ensures a speedy service.

At this point your luggage will be weighed and ticketed. In most airports you can remain in your own wheelchair until embarkation. However, at some airports you may be asked to transfer from your own wheelchair, which will be checked in as baggage to be stowed in the hold. If you do transfer, remember to label all removable parts of your chair and hold on to your cushion if you want to use it on the aircraft seat or avoid losing it in the hold. Some people also keep the removable parts of their wheelchair (ie footrests, side-arms) and take them on board to avoid any possibility of their being mislaid *en route*. If it creates intolerable discomfort to be transferred from your own wheelchair to the airport wheelchair (or if you just do not want to!) you can request to remain in your own chair until boarding. The handling staff may not like this but there is no real reason why you should not wheel yourself through the necessary controls to the aircraft. If you want to visit the Duty Free shop, you will need your airline ticket and boarding pass. Tell whoever may be wheeling you if you wish to make a stop, as sometimes they are keen to whisk you straight past it! One of the advantages of remaining in your own chair until boarding is that you can wheel yourself around the Departure Lounge. Once you transfer into one of the airport chairs you cannot push yourself around because there are brakes which are operated from the back of the chair. You may also want to take the opportunity to visit the wheelchair-accessible toilet in the Departure Lounge and this could be difficult in one of the airport chairs as the side arms are not removable.

Getting On and Off The Aircraft

Facilities to get you on and off the plane vary from airport to airport. In some cases you will be transferred from the terminal building by special vehicle and carried up the airport steps in a carrying chair. Some have a fork lift vehicle available which will lift you up to the aircraft door. If it is a jetty loading plane you will be transferred from your own wheelchair into a narrow push chair that can pass down the aisle to your seat. If you want a special seat on the aircraft, perhaps located directly behind the bulkhead where there is more leg room, an aisle seat, or one close to the toilet, you must request this at the check-in counter. Otherwise seats are allocated on a first-come, first-served basis. Specify whether you wish to smoke or not.

Services for wheelchair users world-wide have steadily improved but in some countries embarking and disembarking from the aircraft can prove to be something of a hair-raising experience.

Equipment may be out-of-date or there may be no special device for lifting you on and off the aircraft, or conveying you to the airport building, so it is left to baggage handlers with no special experience of lifting techniques to get you off the plane and into your own or the airline's wheelchair and wheel you to the airport building. Check with the airline or travel agency before you go about facilities available at the airport of your destination. Usually a member of the cabin staff has to remain with you until you are taken off the aircraft. This could give you the opportunity of explaining how you need to be lifted and, assuming he or she speaks English, the message should get through. If you are worried about the disembarking procedure, try carrying a phrase card in the various languages likely to be encountered which says, for example, 'I cannot walk and my own wheelchair must be retrieved for use at the cabin door'.

Taking Wheelchairs Abroad By Plane

Each airline differs in its policy on carrying electric wheelchairs and you should check with its Passenger Services Department well in advance if you want to take your electric wheelchair, complete with batteries, away with you. If the carrier agrees over the telephone to your taking your electric wheelchair and batteries, then ask for consent in writing in case of any dispute at the check-in desk.

It is important that you or your travelling companion are familiar with the disconnection of the power on your electric wheelchair so that the airline staff can be properly instructed. Most airlines will carry electric wheelchairs free of charge, providing certain conditions are met. Their major fear is an acid spillage from the batteries.

The criteria is usually:

- that the electric wheelchair folds
- that the batteries are emptied of acid or enclosed in an acid-proof container
- that dry cell batteries are disconnected and the battery terminals insulated to prevent short circuiting.

Some airlines will carry electric wheelchairs provided they can be stored upright. Batteries can remain attached providing they are well secured, the terminals disconnected, leads taped down and caps done up tightly.

You might consider leaving the battery behind and obtaining another one at your destination, but this is an expensive option. If you simply cannot manage without your electric chair on holiday, check with the manufacturer about using it abroad, but do this well in advance, as you may need to purchase a voltage converter, plug adaptor, or battery charger. Remember that the power consumption requirements for charging up batteries will vary in different countries.

The Department of Health has no objection to a wheelchair being taken abroad providing that the user accepts full responsibility for the cost of transportation and any repairs that may be required while the wheelchair is out of the country. Wheelchairs, whether electric or manual, can be lost or damaged during transit abroad, so it is always advisable to take out adequate insurance.

As a result of campaigning by the Spinal Injuries Association you do not need to obtain permission to take a non-powered wheelchair abroad on holiday, but if you are leaving the country for six months or more the Department of Health will want to know as, technically, any Government issued chair remains its property. This does not, of course, apply to privately owned wheelchairs.

ON THE AIRCRAFT

Using the Aircraft Toilet

Mobility within the aircraft is not usually possible for a traveller in a wheelchair, although some airlines stow a transit wheelchair on board which is narrow enough to go down the aisle. The width of aisles can be as little as 15 inches on some aircraft, so the transit wheelchair is very narrow indeed.

On long haul flights some airlines do have a 'Streamliner' available for disabled passengers who cannot walk to the toilet. British Airways, for example, has a Streamliner (seat width 16 in) which will take you down the aisle to the lavatory. But do check before you fly that this facility is available on your flight and make sure you are confident about being able to use it. From the Streamliner you will have to transfer backwards on to the toilet seat through the fold-down back rest, otherwise you may need an able-bodied companion to help you to transfer to the toilet. Some airlines have a larger toilet cubicle which will allow a sideways transfer, using the removable arm. British Airways is incorporating a larger lavatory compartment on its 747s for long haul flights. Although this larger cubicle still measures only 62 x 26 in; at least it will allow a travelling companion to offer some assistance in the loo. Disabled travellers who want to empty drainage bags or use a urinal can use the airline's Streamliner to reach the privacy of the WC cubicle, and thereby avoid an embarrassing struggle under the gaze of other passengers. Another advantage is the ability to reach the sink and have a wash and brush up before landing.

Aircraft crew will not be able to assist you in the toilet but they will help you transfer from your seat into the Streamliner and push you down the aisle. Manoeuvrability inside the toilet cubicle will still be minimal and so you will have to be fairly adept at both transferring yourself without the aid of grab rails and adjusting your clothing without help. The toilets on aircraft are not designed to take disabled people, but the Streamliner has been designed to fit into the cubicle, so a compromise, of sorts, has been reached.

If you decide you can manage the Streamliner, then it is advisable to let the air crew know that you intend to use it at some point during your journey so that they can bring it to you at a convenient time and when the aircraft toilets are not too busy. Verify when booking that there is one on board, otherwise you may be in trouble if you are relying upon it. For this reason you would be well advised to take your usual precautions, so that if you decide that using the aircraft lavatory and the Streamliner are too much of a hassle then there are alternative methods which get round the problem. Whatever method you use on board the aircraft - whether by medication or protective incontinence garments, (especially if they are new to you), it is always best to try them out in the safety of your home. It could be disastrous to find out in mid-Atlantic that they do not work.

On shorter routes and charter flights,'on-board' wheelchairs are not available but a seat as close to the toilet as possible can be requested.

Protective Incontinence Aids

Disabled male passengers may not experience too many problems when flying as they can use their usual method of condom and drainage bag, remembering to take a suitable emptying container on board in their hand luggage. One disabled traveller tells us that he uses a double drainage bag system introduced by Convenne when travelling by air and which has got him out of all sorts of difficult situations. He uses a Convenne leg bag No. 5170 (600 ml) with an adjustable tube and the second bag fits straight into the extension on the outlet. If a 1500 ml bag is used many hours of travel should be possible before emptying is necessary.

For females it is a more difficult question which requires a certain amount of thought. Protective pants and extra padding is an option if the air flight is not too long. Further advice on the various types of protective pads and pants can be obtained from the SIA Welfare Office or from the Incontinence Adviser at the Disabled Living Foundation.

Medication

Probanthene is very effective and will help to dry you up, but do take medical advice on this beforehand as it can have side effects, such as nausea and lightheadedness. It is also dangerous to dehydrate yourself too much. A new drug is now available called Desopressin (DDVAP), used in the form of a nasal spray to reduce the amount of urine. Once again, consult your doctor and ask about contra-indications. Bowel management is best dealt with by a sensible approach to eating while on board and sticking to a low-residue diet. If you feel your bowels may let you down during a long flight, there are several medications which you can buy over the chemist's counter, such as Codeine Phosphate or Imodium, (consult your doctor about this and what suits you best), which can be taken several hours before you fly. They are designed to counteract diarrhoea and will dry you up sufficiently to cope with a long flight.

Indwelling Catheter

Some people may decide to use an indwelling catheter while travelling. This should be inserted a couple of days before the flight to make sure it is working properly and that you are familiar with emptying the bag. The local District Nurse attached to the doctor's surgery will usually oblige, if you cannot put it in yourself, and also bring you spare drainage bags, etc.

If the correct sterile procedure is observed, infection should not occur, but of course there is always a risk of infection creeping in and those who do not usually use indwelling catheters would be wise to carry with them a course of antibiotics, just in case!

If you have to empty the bag while in flight use a screw top plastic container which you can either tuck in your hand luggage when full, and empty at your destination, or, give to your travelling companion to empty in the aircraft toilet.

If you are worried about wetting the aircraft seat, remember to sit on your own cushion, on top of which you can place a small plastic sheet or cover. Finally, if anxiety about how you or your bladder will cope on a long flight is putting you off flying for the first time, the Spinal Injuries Association has some useful tips gleaned from its own members' experiences. Members of the Spinal Injuries Association can be linked up with other members who are experienced travellers for personal advice and reassurance.

Comfort in the Air

There are a few points to bear in mind when flying to ensure your own comfort. Make sure the clothes you choose to travel in are loose and comfortable and that your shoes, in particular, are not too tight. This is because due to the pressure in the aircraft cabin, feet tend to swell on long flights.

During the aircraft's descent, pressure within the aircraft cabin changes and this can cause 'popping ears' which can be mildly unpleasant. To alleviate this, try moving the jaw from side to side, sucking a boiled sweet, chewing gum, yawning or swallowing. If these should fail, pinch the end of your nose and with your mouth shut, blow hard or swallow to relieve the pressure.

If you are suffering from a cold, the symptoms will be exaggerated because of the pressure, so don't forget to take a nasal decongestant spray on board if you are suffering from blocked sinuses or a cold at the time of flying.

You may experience sharp changes in temperature, so have a jumper handy in your luggage under the seat.

Air travel can cause disruption of many physiological and psychological rhythms. Rapid transit across several time zones outstrips the body's ability to readjust, and once the body's rhythms are out of synch, jet lag follows. Symptoms include general discomfort, reduced mental and physical performance, altered bowel habits and disrupted appetite. Westward travel is better tolerated by the body than eastward travel. Recovery from jet lag is quick, usually taking only about a day for each time zone crossed. Some seasoned travellers have their own remedies to jet lag - one suggestion is to cut a sole-shape out of brown paper and fit it into your shoe (either foot), leaving it there throughout the flight! Whether this bizarre idea works has not been confirmed, so take more conventional precautions such as sleeping on the plane, avoiding heavy meals and excessive alcohol. A good tip is to make sure that the fresh air vents directly above your seat are open and directed at your face.

Most airlines will provide vegetarian food or any special diet needed if ordered in advance (make sure you state your requirements when booking your flight) and if you are a tetraplegic and unable to unwrap fiddly pre-packed foods you may prefer a sandwich and fresh fruit to airline food.

Escorts

Some airlines such as Pan Am and TWA do not usually allow disabled passengers who cannot use the cabin toilet or eat unaided to travel without an escort. British Airways, however, will allow unaccompanied disabled travellers to fly, provided it is satisfied with the arrangements they have made about using, or not using, the aircraft toilet.

Further advice about travelling comfortably can be obtained from British Airways Medical Service at Heathrow and British Caledonian Airways Medical Centre at Gatwick.

Brittania Airways will provide passengers with any information required about journeys on its aircraft. Contact the Customer Service Department, Luton (0582) 424155 or the Information Desk at Luton Airport (0582) 405100.

British Midland Airways Customer Services will also provide information to passengers who contact them on (0332) 810741 ext 614. Disabled passengers can also contact the East Midlands Airport Information Desk on (0332) 810621.

AIR TRAVELLERS' DIRECTORY-USEFUL ADDRESSES

- **Disabled Living Foundation**
  380/384 Harrow Road
  London W9 2HU
  Tel: 071-289 6111

  Aids and Equipment Centre - permanent exhibition of aids and equipment including the 'Streamliner' chair which airlines use for going up and down aisles which can be tried out and viewed, by appointment. DLF also runs an Incontinent Advisory Service for advice on incontinence products and a Clothing Advisory Service for advice on clothing.

- **Newton Products**
  Meadway Works
  Garretts Green Lane
  Birmingham B33 0SQ
  Tel: 021-783 6081

  Manufacturer of the 'Streamliner'

- **London Regional Transport**
  Travel Information Service
  55 Broadway
  London SW1H 0Bd
  Tel: 071-222 1234 (24-hour service)

- **Air Transport Users Committee**
  2nd Floor Kingsway House
  103 Kingsway
  London WC2B 6
  Tel: 071-242 3882

  National Consumer Organisation for improving facilities for all air transport users. General advice to disabled passengers and booklet ***Care in the Air***

- **Tripscope**
  63 Esmond Road
  Chiswick
  London W4 1JE
  Tel: 081-994 9294

  Information on journey planning

TRAVEL TIP

Some disabled travellers use wheelchairs with a metal zip running the length of the back of the chair. If you feel this idea could help you on your travels then your local Disabled Living Centre can do this for you. Otherwise a wheelchair narrower is an indispensable tool.

CHAPTER SEVEN

TRAVELLING BY RAIL

ACCESS TO THE STATION

British Rail says that its aim is to give disabled people the opportunity to travel by rail as confidently and as independently as possible. With this in mind the needs of disabled travellers are now considered when designing new facilities or refurbishing old stations and rolling stock. BR has equipped over 60 principal stations serving major centres with good access for disabled travellers. The kind of facilities you can expect to find at these stations are conveniently sited car parking spaces, dropped kerbs at station entrances, signs to indicate the easiest routes, 'call for assistance' facilities, wheelchair-accessible toilets equipped with the NKS (National Key Scheme) lock, lifts, access to catering facilities, medium-level pay phones and portable ramps to allow wheelchairs on to the train. Some mainline stations may also have access to long stay car parks but these are not always convenient for wheelchair users as they are sometimes sited some distance from the station. British Rail has a total of 2700 stations around the country and of course, not all of these (some of which are very small indeed) are equipped to cater for disabled passengers. At some older stations access for wheelchair users is likely to be limited, if not impossible, and some local stations are unstaffed, or only staffed at certain times of the day.

However, BR says that many secondary stations are being upgraded with priority given to low-cost improvements such as dropped kerbs at entrances for wheelchair users. If you need a substantial amount of assistance you should consider lengthening your journey by driving to a mainline station where you know access and assistance will be available. Further details of access and facilities at over 400 stations are given in ***Travelling with British Rail - A Guide for Disabled People***.

MAKING ADVANCE ARRANGEMENTS

BR is willing to make special arrangements to look after disabled travellers and it is always best to give the Station Manager advance warning of your arrival so that station staff can assist you and tell you the best place to park, either short or long term. Plan your journey well in advance so that where help is needed it can be arranged. Ideally BR says that it would like two days advance notice if any assistance is required, but sometimes this just is not possible. However, even a few hours notice is helpful. Assistance may be needed, for instance, where platforms at stations cannot be reached by an accessible ramp or lift; when BR staff have to take you by a circuitous route normally reserved for parcels and mail; on Intercity routes when removal of a train seat for a wheelchair user is necessary, or when changing trains during the journey.

Sometimes it goes against the grain for disabled travellers to ask for help, but swallowing your pride is better than being stranded on the station. BR says that if it is not advised in advance, it cannot guarantee being able to provide the level of service hoped for by a disabled traveller. If you decide you do need special arrangements or assistance when you travel, contact the local Area Manager's office by letter or telephone giving the following information:

- date of travel and departure time of trains
- destination station and any intermediate stations *en route* where a change of train is necessary
- if you are a wheelchair user on the InterCity Service, so that seat and table can be removed for you
- any assistance required, eg parking place, help getting out of car or taxi, whether

you can push your own wheelchair, help boarding and leaving the train, etc.

This information should also be provided for the return journey.

If you need any help in planning your journey, contact the local Area Manager's office, asking for the person who deals with travel for disabled passengers. Alternatively, ring the number listed in your telephone directory under British Rail - Passenger Train Service Information.

TRANSPORT TO AND FROM THE STATION

If you are planning to take a taxi from one of the London mainline stations, only licensed London cabs are available without prior arrangement. The traditional 'London style' taxi can be difficult to use, especially with a wheelchair plus luggage. However, there are now several hundred new Metrocabs available for hire which are completely accessible; a person in a wheelchair can be pushed up a ramp into the side door and travel in the wheelchair. Metrocabs can be booked up to three days in advance by ringing 071-286 2728 (ask for LIFT bookings). If you have a taxicard ring 071-286 0666. Computer Cab have 12 Metrocabs and some FX4Ws which have been adapted to enable a person to travel in a wheelchair but you must book four days in advance. Taxi Trade promotions also operate a 'book ahead' system. If phoning from the station try Data Cab, Black Cabs, Lords Radio Taxis, and Metro Cabs, all of whom operate wheelchair-accessible taxis.

At large mainline stations, the likelihood of finding a wheelchair-accessible black cab is good. A porter will direct you to the taxi rank and if there is not an adapted cab available, one of the other taxi drivers can use his radio to summon one to the rank.

Londoners can join the Taxicard scheme, whereby people with disabilities who are unable to use conventional public transport can use London taxis (black cabs) at a substantially reduced rate, for example, £7-worth of taxi travel for £1 flat fare. To qualify for the scheme you must be a resident of a London borough and in receipt of Mobility Allowance, War Pensioners' Mobility Supplement, be a registered blind person, or produce a letter from your doctor stating that you are unable to use public transport because you have a permanent disability. The London Taxicard scheme does not apply to the boroughs of Barnet, Redbridge and the City of Westminster, which operate their own similar schemes. In Edinburgh, a Taxicard scheme operates for permanent residents. For more information about the Taxicard scheme contact the Unit for Disabled Passengers, LRT.

Dial-A-Ride is a door-to-door transport scheme for people living in London who cannot use public transport. You may be able to take advantage of the Dial-A-Ride service if you are a member and there is a scheme operating in your area, although there are some restrictions on how far the Dial-A-Ride can take you. Most schemes travel only within the borough and neighbouring districts. Remember to book well in advance of your travel date and also take into consideration the need for punctuality when running to a strict timetable with a train to catch. To find out about the local Dial-A-Ride service contact the London Dial-A-Ride Users Association.

Outside London, most areas have some form of voluntary transport available to take you or pick you up from the station, such as that run by local community transport schemes, the British Red Cross, or WRVS, but, once again, you will have to make arrangements for this well in advance.

Some Useful Addresses

- **London Dial-A-Ride Users Association**
  St Margarets
  25 Leighton Road
  London NW5 2QD
  Tel: 071-482 2325

- **Taxicard Section**
  London Regional Transport
  55 Broadway
  London SW1H 0BD

Tel: 071-222 5600 or 071-227 3588 - direct line for Taxicard scheme; application form and information booklet available.

Wheelchair-accessible taxi firms

- **Computer Cab**
  7 Woodfield Road
  London W9 ZBA

  Metro and Fairway accessible black cabs
- **Computer Cab**
  Taxicard Book Ahead
  Tel: 071-286 7009
- **Computer Cab**
  Suburban Areas
  Tel: 081-940 1594 or 081-445 0022
- **Taxi Trade Promotions**
  431 Caledonian Road
  Islington
  London N7 9BG
  Tel: 071-700 5681

  Fleet of Fairway accessible cabs - book 1 week in advance
- **Black Radio Taxis**
  Tudor House
  Llanvanor Road
  Golders Green
  London NW 2AR
  Tel: 081-209 0266

  Metro and Fairway cabs
- **Dial-A-Cab**
  24 Skyline Village
  Lime Harbour, E14
  Tel: 071-253 5000

Accessible taxis outside the London area

- **Ace Taxis**
  16 Emery Road
  Brislington
  Bristol 4
  Tel: (0272) 777477
  (0272) 774777

  Book 2-3 days in advance
- **City Centre Cabs**
  132 Bute Street
  The Docks
  Cardiff
  Tel: (0222) 488888
- **HRH Taxis**
  29 Osprey Park
  Thornbury
  Avon
  Tel: (0454) 414179

USING THE UNDERGROUND

Travelling across any big city on the Underground is usually not a viable option for wheelchair users. London Regional Transport (LRT) says it will do all it can to help you use the Underground and if you use a wheelchair LRT can make arrangements for you to use the sub-surface, Circle, District, East London and Metropolitan lines outside peak travelling hours. However, it does not consider the 'deep' central London lines to be safe for people in wheelchairs because of evacuation difficulties in the event of train failures or accidents. The majority of the London Underground stations have flights of steps or escalators and are inaccessible to travellers using wheelchairs. Some stations do have lifts but these are usually only reached by means of stairs or an escalator. More details about the accessibility or otherwise of London stations is given in a booklet ***Access to the Underground*** available from the Unit for Disabled Passengerrs, LRT.

In most large cities the Underground railway systems are generally inaccessible to people using wheelchairs. However, there are exceptions; the Tyne and Wear Metro system was designed to be fully accessible and has special interchanges with parking bays for disabled travellers as well as general access to bus stations. The Docklands Light Railway is also fully accessible to wheelchair travellers. Lifts or ramps are provided to all platforms, and the trains have space for wheelchairs. A leaflet ***Access to the Docklands Light Railway*** is available from LRT's Unit for Disabled Passengers.

INTERCITY TRAINS

The InterCity trains serving the main rail network are nearly all accessible. They are equipped with wide access doors, grab rails, self-opening interior doors and accommodation for wheelchairs in the existing 125 stock. One snag is that the doorway between the vestibule and the seating area is only 26in wide and the arm of the seat opposite the wheelchair space protrudes some two inches into the doorway opening, so if you use a standard Everest & Jennings or Carters wheelchair for example, you will have to take a wheelchair narrower with you or be capable of pulling yourself up on the door frame while a porter or companion half folds the chair beneath you and pushes it through the opening. A single seat and table at one end of a first class coach are removed to allow you to sit in your own wheelchair. The table is too low to be used by a person seated in a standard wheelchair, being 25 inches above ground level, so you will be unable to tuck your knees comfortably underneath. In the latest standard coaches seats without tables close to the entrance are designated for disabled travellers.

BR says that 80 per cent of InterCity coaches now have space for wheelchair users to travel in the passenger saloon and in the future, with new trains being developed, there will be enough room for two people in wheelchairs to travel together and sit either side of the aisle within talking distance, not in separate compartments as before.

On-train toilets for passengers in wheelchairs are being installed in the vestibule area of all new InterCity trains. The vestibules have been designed with clear access so there are no barricades or obstacles preventing access to the toilet. Several existing coaches serving the London - Glasgow route have this facility, but if you are travelling on another route and know you will need to use the lavatory sometime during the trip, the only alternative is to break your journey somewhere *en route* and use the wheelchair-accessible toilet on the station (make sure before you alight that this facility is available).

Unfortunately, this break to find an accessible 'comfort station' will probably delay your journey by at least an hour, by which time you may be needing the facility again ..... It makes most sense to give up drinking before and during your trip.

British Rail is proposing to convert all its wheelchair-accessible toilets at stations, (the majority of which will be Unisex in future), to National Key Scheme locks, so if you intend using the railway network you would benefit by joining the scheme. Keys, together with a list of all the wheelchair-accessible toilets in the scheme, are available from RADAR. Disabled toilet facilities are being included in all newly built mainline stock. When this brand new and accessible on-train facility was introduced by BR some years ago, SIA and other organisations were invited to travel on the trial run from Euston to Manchester to test it thoroughly. SIA members who tried this new innovative facility gave it the 'thumbs-up' and, apart from a few minor points, look forward to its introduction on all InterCity trains. Although the toilet cubicle is small it is so well designed that a wheelchair user has just enough room to manoeuvre in, close the door and use the loo. There are grab rails alongside the toilet and a conveniently sited handbasin. There is also just enough room for a determined helper to squeeze in to render assistance if required.

The internal doors connecting coaches on existing rolling stock can be a problem to a disabled traveller, as the wheelchair is probably too wide to go through the doorway. This makes it impossible to gain access to different coaches, for example, the dining car, where a seat, but not a removable one, can be reserved in advance. For those unable to reach the restaurant, meals and snacks can be served at their seats.

On the older types of InterCity trains there are no special facilities for disabled travellers and, because of the design of the coaches, people in wheelchairs who cannot use the passenger areas will, therefore, have to travel in the guard's van.

LOCAL SERVICES

On local cross-country services, almost all the existing stock of multiple units will have been replaced by sliding-door coaches within the next five years. Wide door openings and low floor levels give easy access to all, including wheelchair users. Wherever possible on longer distance journeys, BR plans to install toilet facilities for passengers in wheelchairs.

On the provincial services where on-train toilets are planned these will comply with the wheelchair access specification, but on some of the shorter-distance provincial services it is just not practical to install any toilet facilities. In London and the South-East commuter areas, some existing 'slam door' stock with narrow doorways has, unfortunately, a long life expectancy, and rebuilding to admit wheelchairs is not possible either financially or structurally. Hence, many guard's vans are being upgraded to provide a more comfortable environment for wheelchair travellers and their companions who are unable to enter the passenger coaches. On provincial service stock access to the carriage will be by sliding doors (like those used on tube trains) which are easily accessible to wheelchair users. There will be a convertable area in one of the coaches with flip-up seats for longer journeys, allowing a passenger in a wheelchair to slot in and sit with their companions throughout the journey. For shorter journeys passengers using wheelchairs can position themselves in the vestibule area, where there is plenty of room.

DISABLED PERSONS' RAILCARD

If you intend to do a lot of travelling on the BR network, then along with your RADAR key for the unisex loos, you would be well advised to buy a Disabled Persons' Railcard. These are available to permanently and severely disabled people, such as those in receipt of the Mobility Allowance. The Railcard allows you and a companion half-rate day return fares, or 34 per cent off other fares. A Railcard costs £12 and is valid for 12 months from date of purchase.

If you do not hold a Railcard there are still some reductions on the standard fare for yourself and one travelling companion. A free leaflet and information about the Disabled Persons' Railcard and other concessionary fares for the disabled called ***British Rail and Disabled Travellers*** is available from your local British Rail Station or from the British Railways Board.

RAIL TRAVELLERS' DIRECTORY- USEFUL ADDRESSES (UK)

- **British Railways Board**
  (Central Publicity Unit)
  Mulberry House
  Marylebone
  London NW1

  Issues leaflets ***Disabled Persons Railcard - Getting There Cheaper*** & ***British Rail and Disabled Travellers***

- **London Underground**
  London Regional Transport (LRT)
  Unit for Disabled Passengers
  55 Broadway
  London SW1H 0BD
  Tel: 071-237 3312

Access to the Underground (price 70p)
A guide for disabled people

- **Tyne & Wear Passenger Transport Executive**
  Marketing & Information Office
  Cuthbert House
  All Saints
  Newcastle upon Tyne NE1 2DA

  Travel Line passenger information
  Tel: 091-232 5325

- **RADAR**
  25 Mortimer Street
  London W1N 8AB
  Tel: 071-637 5400
  National Key Scheme

  Key and list of toilets fitted with the NKS Lock for disabled people including those operated by BR

- **Department of Transport**
  Victoria Road
  South Ruislip
  Middlesex HA4 ONZ

  Publishes a transport guide for people with disabilities.

RAIL TRAVEL ABROAD

Rail travel in the USA

Access Amtrak

For many people with disabilities, rail travel offers a comfortable and attractive alternative to other forms of transportation. Visitors to the States can sit back and enjoy the scenery in comfort on the National Railroad Passenger Corporation, more commonly known as Amtrak, America's only InterCity rail service which operates throughout the United States and Canada. It has some excellent services to offer disabled passengers.

Since the degree of accessibility of Amtrak's different types of coaches and stations varies, it is important for disabled travellers to determine whether Amtrak can meet their needs. If you are travelling in America, all you need to do is call the toll-free operator, if possible 24 hours in advance of travelling, on (800) and ask for USA-RAIL and then the Special Service Desk. Amtrak can then arrange help with your wheelchair, baggage, and where necessary assist with boarding. All Amtrak's new stations have been built to be fully accessible to people in wheelchairs and many of the older stations have been renovated and modifications made for partial, if not full, accessibility.

There are two types of Amtrak services which have very good access, the Superliner and the Metroliner. The Metroliner is Amtrak's hourly high-speed service between Washington DC and New York which stops at high-level platforms that provide level entry into the train. Each car is equipped with a wheelchair-accessible toilet and nearby seat with storage space for a wheelchair. The wide spaced seating means there is plenty of room to transfer from your wheelchair into a comfortable seat with ample leg room.

Amtrak's Superline service offers long distance routes on trains with double-decker carriages designed with special features for disabled travellers in both coach and sleeping cars. Access to the coaches is via a ramp from the station carried on each car.

On the older Heritage Fleet, accessible sleeping accommodation for disabled passengers is called a roomette, and comes with its own toilet and washing facilities. There is a wheelchair lifting device to assist with boarding, as these older carriages have steep steps.

In the next decade all the older trains are being replaced with Viewliner carriages. Sleepers, complete with wheelchair-accessible toilets and showers, and fully accessible dining car, have already been designed. A prototype Viewliner currently operates on the overnight train between Boston and Washington DC.

On some of the services, Amtrak offers 25 per cent off the regular one-way coach fare for travellers with disabilities, if they cannot fully use the Amtrak services.

For further information about Amtrak's routes and services, a copy of the National Timetable, and ***Amtrak's America***, an

89-page travel planner that includes information for disabled passengers, write to:

- **Amtrak Distribution Centre**
  PO Box 7717
  Itasca
  IL 60143
  USA

For information about access in New York City on the subway system and on wheelchair-accessible buses, write for a copy of ***The Guide to Riding Wheelchair-Accessible Buses in NYC*** to:

- **Barrier Free Design Department**
  Eastern Paralysed Veterans Association
  75-20 Astoria Boulevard
  Jackson Heights
  NY 11370-1178
  USA

Rail travel in Canada

The older stock used on the Canadian railways is not easily accessible to travellers using wheelchairs, but the new LRC (Light, Rapid and Comfortable) train which serves Quebec City, Montreal, Ottawa, Kingston, Toronto, London and Windsor does have suitable facilities. Disabled travellers can either transfer to a coach seat or remain in their own wheelchairs and there is a wheelchair tie-down in some club cars. A wheelchair-accessible toilet is found in close proximity to the designated seat. Advance notice is necessary to ensure a tie-down wheelchair spot and a car with an accessible toilet.

Rail Canada offer a Two-for-One fare to a disabled traveller and a companion who is capable of rendering assistance upon production of an identification card which can be obtained from the Canadian Rehabilitation Council for the Disabled.

Rail Canada publish a guide ***Travel Tips for Passengers with Special Needs*** which gives further information on special facilities. Write to:

- **Rail Canada Inc**
  Head Office
  2 Place Ville Marie
  Montreal
  Quebec H3B 4M9
  Canada

or

- **Rail Canada**
  Thomas Cook Ltd
  PO Box 36
  Thorpewood
  Peterborough PE3 6SB

- **Canadian Rehabilitation Council for the Disabled (CRCD)**
  One Young Street
  Suite 2110
  Toronto
  Ontario M5E 1E5

Rail travel in Europe

Rail services for disabled people vary greatly throughout Europe. For example, France has a very advanced rail system and good facilities for disabled travellers, while in some countries little provision is made. Below are some of the countries which do provide services and facilities for disabled travellers.

Austria A lightweight portable chair is used to lift disabled people on to the train and for manoeuvreing within the train.

Belgium There are some special facilities for disabled travellers at some railway stations. For further information contact Belgium National Railways, Permia House, 10 Greycoat Place, London W1X 1ED
Tel: 071-233 0360

Denmark For information on the services offered for disabled travellers contact the Danish State Railways, Solvgade 40, DK-1307, Copenhagen K, Denmark

France There is good access for wheelchair travellers at many railway stations in France and most of the major stations have a wheelchair-accessible toilet.

On the super fast TGV trains special areas have been reserved for wheelchair travellers and some accessible Corail coaches use the Paris-Nice route. On many major stations boarding and deboarding is by an electrically operated vertical transfer device which lifts disabled travellers on and off the train. On some routes wheelchair users can remain in their wheelchairs for the journey. On board some trains there are small wheelchairs which can manoeuvre down aisles to the dining car.

The French Railways issues ***Guide Pratique due Voyageur - supplement a l'intention des personnes a mobilete reduite***. It is, of course, printed in French and is available from mainline stations in France.

Germany ***Reisefuhrer fur unsere Behindernten Fahrgaste*** (printed in German) gives information about access to stations and facilities on trains for disabled people. Available from most German mainline stations or Zentral Verkaufsleitung, Deutsche Bundesbahn, Rhabanusstrasse 3, 3-6500, Mainz, W Germany.

Holland The Nederland Railway (Nederlandse Spoorwgen - NS) has a special telephone number that disabled travellers can dial from Monday - Friday 8.30am to 4pm (030 331253) which gives information on services and facilities available.

Norway The Norwegian State Railway has introduced a special railway carriage equipped with a hydraulic lifting platform and a specially adapted compartment for wheelchair travellers. There is also a wheelchair-accessible toilet on board.

Further information from Norwegian State Railways, 21-24 Cockspur Street, London SW1Y 5DA.
Tel: 071-930 6666

Sweden Information available about the Swedish State Railways from the UK agent, the Norwegian State Railway at the above address.

Switzerland On the new InterCity trains, disabled travellers can remain in their wheelchairs but on older stock travel is in the guard's van.

CHAPTER EIGHT

TRAVELLING BY ROAD

For those who drive, a hand-controlled car is probably the single greatest aid to independence, but whether you are the driver or the navigator, a motoring holiday on the Continent can be an exhilarating and rewarding experience, provided you follow the advice in this chapter on Continental driving and have packed all the essentials.

MOTORING ON THE CONTINENT

Driving on the Continent should cause you no problems, as long as you are cautious. Do not overdo it; people often have accidents because they aim to travel too far in one day, become tired and lose concentration. Motoring laws in Europe are just as complicated as those in the UK but they should cause little difficulty to the average British motorist who drives carefully and remembers the essentials of good motoring.

Rules of the road

In most European countries you must drive on the right and overtake on the left. Driving on the right-hand side of the road may sound like a nightmare, but it is surprising how quickly you adjust. There will be plenty of signs to remind you to drive on the right as soon as you leave the port or airport. Take it slowly at first, especially at roundabouts and traffic intersections, and you will soon be driving like a native. Take special care to drive on the right when leaving petrol stations or cafés (especially if they are situated on the left-hand side of the road), after a few hours stop *en route* or when you leave your hotel or holiday accommodation the next day. Some drivers stick a notice on their windscreen to remind them, or rely upon the front-seat passenger to jog their memory every time they make a fresh start. Always pay attention to the local speed limits and the rules of the road.

Road conditions

You may find when driving on the Continent that the roads are not as busy as they are in the UK. Main roads are usually in good condition but the camber is often steeper than is usually found in the UK and the edges of some roads may be jagged and uneven. In France signposts saying ***Chausee deformee*** are sometimes posted to warn motorists of this hazard. Where roads are closed for repairs, you will often find signs alerting you to any diversions. In France this is ***deviation*** and in Germany ***Umleitung***.

Lights

For driving abroad headlights should be adjusted so that the dipped beam does not light the wrong side of the road and dazzle oncoming traffic. The adjustment can be made by fitting beam converters or deflectors, available from your local motor accessory shop or AA Centre. Dipped headlights should also be used in bad weather conditions, such as heavy rain, and when driving through a tunnel, irrespective of its length and degree of lighting. In some countries police will wait at the end of a tunnel to check that motorists are complying with this requirement.

Road signs

These are mainly international these days and so you should be familiar with the majority of them, which makes driving on the Continent much easier for everyone. There are, however, a few road signs peculiar to specific countries, but these are listed in literature from the major 'clubs'. You should particularly watch for signs indicating crossings and speed limits. Probably the most disconcerting aspect of driving abroad to the British motorist is the universal and firm rule giving priority to traffic coming from the right and unless this rule is varied by signs, it must be strictly observed.

Overtaking

Driving on the Continent means you are sitting on the 'blind' side of the car. Pulling out to overtake can be risky and a useful aid, if you cannot rely on a fellow traveller is the 'Co-pilot Overtaking Mirror' which gives you left-hand drive vision of the road. When overtaking on roads with two lanes or more in each direction, always signal your intention in good time, and after the manoeuvre, signal and return to the inside lane. Do not remain in any other lane. Failure to comply with this regulation, particularly in France, may incur an on-the-spot fine.

Priority at junctions and roundabouts

The general rule is to give way to traffic approaching a junction from the right, but this is sometimes varied at roundabouts. (This is an aspect of driving on the Continent which may cause confusion). Road signs indicate priority or loss of priority so drivers must make sure that they understand such signs. Some useful hints to remember when driving in France, for example, are that traffic approaching unsigned roundabouts has priority and at signed roundabouts bearing the words '***vous n'avez pas la priority***' or '***cedez le passage***' traffic already on the roundabout has priority.

Intersections

Great care should be taken at intersections and drivers should never rely on receiving the right of way, particularly in small towns and villages where slow-moving local traffic, such as farm tractors, will assume right of way regardless of oncoming traffic.

Traffic lights

In major cities and towns traffic lights operate in a way similar to those in the UK, although they are sometimes suspended overhead. There is usually only one set on the right-hand side of the road some distance before the road junction, and if you stop too close to the corner the lights will not be visible. Watch out for filter lights which will allow you to turn right at a junction against the main lights. If you wish to go straight ahead do not enter a lane leading to filter lights otherwise you may find yourself taking an unwanted left turn or obstructing traffic waiting to turn left.

Motorways (Autoroutes)

On the Continent, motorways tend to be excellent but expensive. The majority of autoroutes have tolls. Tolls are charged on most motorways in France, Italy, Portugal, Spain and on sections in Austria, Greece and Yugoslavia. Keep some currency and plenty of loose change handy, as Travellers' cheques are not acceptable at toll booths. For a guide to motorway charges see the AA publication ***Hotels and Restaurants in Europe*** which is updated annually. It will give you a rough idea of the cost of using autoroutes which can be expensive. For example, if you are driving in France from one of the Channel ports to the south, the charge for a single journey is around £35. Petrol is also much more expensive on the Continent, particularly on the autoroutes. In Switzerland the authorities charge an annual motorway tax.

Holiday traffic

The months of July and August are the peak of the touring season, particularly in Austria, Belgium, France and Germany when the school holidays start, and during this period motorways and main roads can be heavily congested. If you want to travel on less congested roads during the holiday season (June - September) in France, motorist should follow the 'green arrow' holiday routes. A free road map showing the marked alternative routes, plus information centres and petrol stations open 24 hours is available from service stations displaying the 'Bison Futé' poster (a Red Indian chief).

Accidents and breakdowns

In the event of an accident or breakdown, stop the vehicle and place a warning triangle on the road at a suitable distance to warn following traffic of the obstruction. The use of hazard warning lights does not bypass the regulations governing the use of warning triangles abroad. If the accident is serious report it to the police and notify your insurance company (by letter if possible) within 24 hours of the accident. If a third party is injured, the insurance company whose address is given on the back of your Green Card should be notified. It is a good idea to take photographs if you can, particularly of any other vehicles involved. The law and levels of damages in foreign countries are generally different to our own and it is important to remember this when considering a claim against another motorist after an accident abroad. The negotiation of claims against foreign insurers is extremely long and tedious and translation of all documents slows down the process. A delay of three months between sending a letter and receiving a reply is not uncommon. So drive carefully!

If you are involved in an accident in France you must complete a 'constat à l'amiable', and get it signed by the other party before your vehicle is moved. In Yugoslavia the driver of a vehicle involved in an accident must inform the traffic police immediately and wait for an on-the-spot investigation and written report.

Emergencies

If you are in serious trouble or distress the British Embassy or Consulate of the country you are visiting will help or advise British travellers. More information about the type of help the British Consulate abroad can give can be found in Chapter 10.

Orange Badge scheme - Reciprocal arrangements with European countries

Several European countries operate national parking concession schemes for people with disabilities. Disabled visitors to these countries can enjoy the concessions provided in the host country by displaying the badge of their own scheme. However, in some countries responsibility for introducing the concessions rests with individual local authorities, so they may not be generally available. In such cases badge holders should enquire locally, as they should whenever they are in any doubt as to their entitlement. As in this country, the arrangements apply only to the badge holders themselves. Unfortunately, the scheme does not extend to non-European countries.

There are 12 countries taking part in the scheme; Austria, Belgium, Denmark, Finland, France, West Germany, Italy, Luxembourg, Netherlands, Portugal, Sweden and Switzerland. Concessions vary from one country to another but they usually allow for an extension of the time limit where waiting is restricted and an entitlement to use special parking places reserved for the disabled. A summary of parking concessions available to disabled people in European countries may be obtained from the Department of Transport.

ACCESSIBLE ACCOMMODATION EN ROUTE

Finding accessible hotels *en route* can be a challenge, but throughout most of the Continent there are chains of hotels which have one or more specially designed rooms with an *en suite* bathroom suitable for wheelchair users. The Ibis, Urbis and Novotel chains for example are very helpful and can be booked from the UK through Resinter International Hotel Reservations (Tel: 071-724 1000). If you book by credit card through Resinter you can arrange for your booking to be held for you if you are not sure what time of night you will arrive at your destination. These hotels tend to be a little expensive, but offer fairly comfortable accommodation and there is the added advantage of being able to book them in advance from the UK. They are usually sited close to motorways and near large towns and so are relatively easy to find. However, because of the price, they are really only suitable for overnight stays *en route* to your destination.

The National Tourist Office of the country you are visiting can often provide information about accessible accommodation, as can the country's national disability association, where plenty of information will be available. It might, however, be printed in a foreign language. SIA's Information Service has most access publications issued on the subject, together with details of accessible accommodation tried and tested by SIA members.

Armed with plenty of information and some careful planning comfortable stay-on-the-way accommodation can always be found.

Accessible facilities en route

Accessible restaurants and bars are a little more difficult but not impossible to find. It may be easier to stop at the first level supermarket and buy a picnic of local goodies to eat *en route* if you do not want to spend time hunting for a suitable eating place. Picnic areas on the Continent are plentiful and often quite attractive, with picnic tables set back from the road.

Wheelchair-accessible toilets are not easy to find when you are travelling off the beaten track on the Continent. However, if you are using motorways or autoroutes most service stations have excellent clean wheelchair- accessible facilities.

USEFUL ADDRESSES

International Hotel Chains, which operate throughout Europe and provide specially adapted bedrooms with *en suite* bathrooms for disabled guests (the Novotel, Sofitel and Mecure hotel and motel chain and the Ibis & Urbis Hotels group) issue separate directories which indicate accommodation suitable for disabled people. The directories are available from -

- International Reservations Office
  2nd Floor
  Novotel London
  1 Shortlands
  Hammersmith
  London W6 8DR
  Tel: 071-724 1000

MOTORING ACCESSORIES & PORTABLE AIDS

There are numerous motoring accessories available on the market which can make all the difference towards making driving a comfortable, safe and enjoyable experience, especially on a Continental touring holiday. Most of these accessories can be found in the high street shops, but there are some aids and accessories of particular use to disabled travellers and the names and addresses of manufacturers are listed at the end of this chapter.

Disabled people can join a number of motoring organisations and clubs which amongst other things, are happy to give advice on aids to help disabled drivers and passengers have a successful journey. Most of these organisations also produce their own signs and signals to make motoring for a disabled driver easier. The Disabled Drivers' Association produces a 'Help' pennant made of orange flourescent plastic with the wheelchair symbol which will hang from a car window to attract attention. The Disabled Motorists' Federation has a self-adhesive vinyl sticker for use on the rear windscreen: *Disabled Driver - No Hand Signals,* Mobility International has a yellow and red self-adhesive sticker *Don't park too close - I have to get my wheelchair in* and Inter-Able Aid Ltd manufactures a triangle distress light which is powered by a cigarette lighter and which uses the wheelchair symbol and a large *Help* which it is hoped you will not have to use too often.

A really useful motoring aid, especially if you are motoring abroad, is a 'blind spot' mirror which enables you to have a clear and magnified view of the far right rear of the car if fitted to the driver's side or the far left rear of the car if fitted to the passenger side, or convex mirrors which provide a wide angle panoramic view of the rear of the vehicle and of the road behind.

A helpful accessory for people of below-average height, for whom the sun visor does not extend far enough over the windscreen, is the Robinclay sun shield which fits on to the existing visor and is fully adjustable for see-through and see-under vision.

Steering wheel knobs are often an asset to the disabled driver, as they help to give firm control of the wheel and lessen the strength needed to turn it. They are particularly useful at roundabouts and sharp corners. A steering wheel table serves the same purpose as the knob and hooks over any steering wheel. It can be set at the most convenient angle and locked into position. For personal comfort, an adjustable back rest gives good lumber support and can help with the problem of back ache on a long journey. For many disabled people, sitting for any length of time can be dangerous and lead to pressure sores. Several companies manufacture either real or artificial sheepskin covers which you can place over the seat to provide a friction-free surface. Some disabled drivers or passengers keep a special cushion on the car seat which can be effective in relieving pressure on bony prominences or keeping the rear end cool. These cushions are foam, gel or water-filled and can be expensive, so enquire about obtaining one from your GP, hospital consultant or social services department.

A sliding board is always a useful piece of equipment to carry with you as it can be used in a variety of situations. If you have difficulty getting in and out of your car and have enough strength in your arms, you could invest in a car grip which engages in the roof trough of the car to help you make the transfer from car seat to wheelchair. Inability to get in and out of a car independently is no reason to abandon your travels. There are several lightweight, compact and easy to manoeuvre hoists on the market which can be dismantled and stowed in the boot and require no major alterations to the car.

If you or your travelling companion has severe postural problems and finds sitting in a regular car seat uncomfortable, support seats designed to alleviate pressure points and give postural support are available through the NHS. These seats are suitable for either car or wheelchair and are available on a doctor's referral. Several firms who specialise in adapting cars and providing car accessories for disabled drivers or passengers supply sliding swivel seats as a replacement seat for passenger or driver. These units consist of a bucket seat mounted on a steel platform which fits to the standard seat mountings, replacing the original seat which can be stored and refitted when the car is changed.

Detachable arm rests can be fitted to support the unstable passenger, and there is a range of car seats named 'Contour' designed to overcome discomfort, fatigue and strain. The back of the seat includes an inflatable lumbar air cushion which provides support just where it is needed.

In most countries on the Continent the wearing of seat belts is compulsory. If the prospect of wearing an uncomfortable seat belt is unpleasant, there is a range of quick release safety harnesses available to suit individual needs for both children and disabled adults.

Coach and Bus Travel for Disabled People

In the USA the Greyhound bus service offers a 'helping hand service' which allows a disabled traveller and a companion to travel together on a single ticket. The only requirement is that the travelling companion must be able to provide assistance in the form of help on and off the bus, attend to any needs *en route*, and travel with the disabled person for the complete trip. Travellers using wheelchairs who cannot walk up the steps will have to be carried to their seats as there is no wheelchair access, but Greyhound staff will assist with this.

Many Greyhound terminals have features for disabled travellers such as accessible toilets and food service areas.

To qualify for the two-for-the-price-of-one ticket, the disabled traveller must present a written statement from a doctor stating he or she needs a companion for physical assistance to board, alight and travel on the bus.

For a free brochure, ***Reach for Greyhound's Helping Hand*** write to:

- **Greyhound World Travel**
  Sussex House
  London Road
  East Grinstead
  West Sussex RH19 1LD
  Tel: (0342) 317317

ESSENTIAL DOCUMENTS FOR CONTINENTAL DRIVING

Vehicle Registration Document

Always carry it with you. You will need the actual document, not a photocopy. If your vehicle registration document is at DVLC, Swansea, get a Certificate of Registration (Form V379) from your local vehicle licensing office. Hire vehicles require a Vehicle Hire Certificate (VE103A), obtainable from the AA or RAC. In Portugal this should be accompanied by an officially authenticated photocopy of the registration document. If you plan to borrow a vehicle the registration document must be accompanied by written authorisation. In Yugoslavia this letter of authority must be countersigned by the AA; for Portugal a special certificate is required - available free from the AA.

Driving Licence

Always carry it with you. A full UK licence is valid throughout Europe. Provisional licences are not acceptable.

International Driving Permit

Required for Spain and Eastern Europe.

Insurance - Green Card

It is essential to inform your insurers or broker when you intend to take your vehicle abroad and you should obtain a Green Card (International Motor Insurance Certificate) from them. You should order it at least a month ahead of your intended travel date. UK insurance provides only minimal cover in Europe and will not provide compensation for damage, fire, theft or personal accident. Although it is no longer a legal requirement in EEC countries, it is always advisable to get a Green Card so that you are effectively covered. A Green Card is also accepted as evidence of vehicle insurance in most countries.

A ***Bail Bond*** is strongly recommended for Spain.

Note: There is no time allowed to produce essential documents in Europe as there is in the UK; you will need to produce them on the spot if necessary, so always carry your driving licence, insurance certificate (Green Card) and vehicle registration document with you when driving. Do not leave them in an unattended vehicle.

Find out about the traffic rules and regulations of the country you are visiting at least a month before you go and familiarise yourself with them.

EUROPEAN MOTORING LAWS

GB sticker

Compulsory to display an international distinguishing sign on the back of your car. The ferry company will automatically send you one of the correct dimensions with your ferry tickets.

Warning triangle

Must be used in most European countries when a vehicle has stopped for any reason - not just for breakdowns.

Seat belts

Compulsory to wear them in most European countries.

First aid kit

Wise to carry a first aid kit in your car. In some European countries it is compulsory.

Fire extinguisher

Advisable, and compulsory in some countries, to carry a fire extinguisher in the car.

Headlight bulbs

Compulsory in some European countries, but it is always advisable in any case, to carry a spare set.

Headlights

Adjust headlights to dip to the right. Conversion kits for most makes of cars are available from motor accessory shops.

Mirrors

Most countries require you to have two wing mirrors but a left-hand side mirror is advisable when motoring in Europe.

Insurance

Check with your insurer that your existing motor policy, together with the Green Card, offers adequate cover for all the countries in which you intend to travel. If you want the security of extra services you could contact Europ Assistance which is able to help travellers stranded abroad in over 150 countries. It can provide comprehensive medical, motoring and personal travel insurance cover, both short term (91 days) for holiday or business trips abroad and long term (annual) for frequent travellers abroad. Disabled travellers applying for insurance cover with Europ Assistance receive individual assessment. The company will provide cover for all eventualities that may be encountered by disabled travellers, except expenses resulting from an incident caused by their existing condition. Europ Assistance also runs a 24-hour combined medical emergency service and travel insurance package which provides comprehensive protection for motorists planning to take their car abroad.

For further details -

- **Europ Assistance**
  Europ Assistance House
  252 High Street
  Croydon
  Surrey CR0 1NF
  Tel: 081-680 1234

SOME USEFUL INFORMATION FOR CONTINENTAL DRIVING

Petrol

Make sure you have enough currency to buy petrol or that the petrol station will accept credit cards. Eurocard/Mastercard

(Access), Visa (Barclaycard) and Trustcard are the most widely accepted credit cards used for the purchase of petrol.

Continental leaded petrol has a lower lead content than in the UK which can cause a slight loss of engine power. Unleaded petrol is quite common in some countries so make sure your car can take it. In France it is marked 'essence sans plomb', in Germany 'bleifrei' and in Italy 'Benzina senza di carbonio'.

Petrol prices at filling stations on motorways will be higher than elsewhere while at self-service pumps it will be slightly cheaper. Motorway service stations abroad usually provide 24 hour-service but some smaller garages may close 12 noon-3pm for lunch. Overseas, both leaded and unleaded petrol is graded as Normal and Super. A roof-rack laden with luggage increases petrol consumption, which should be taken into consideration when calculating mileage.

Night driving

It is advisable to use amber headlights when driving on the continent. Either obtain amber lens converters which can be fitted over your headlights or paint on yellow lacquer which is easily removed - available from motor accessory shops.

Spares

Take a few essential spares with you (headlight bulbs, fan belt, etc.). You can hire comprehensive spares kits for your car including emergency windscreen and warning triangle if you do not own them.

Engine chassis number

Keep a note of this as a precaution.

Motorway tolls

Tolls are payable on most European motorways, so have some local currency handy. Tolls are based on the pro-rata distance travelled, and over long distances toll charges can be quite considerable. In Switzerland the authorities charge an annual motorway tax.

Personal Documents

Tickets

Return ferry tickets for you, your passengers and vehicle. Keep them in a safe place - not at home!

Passport

A standard passport valid beyond the date of return is required for all travel abroad.

Visas

These are required for some East European countries. If travelling on a non-British passport check whether you need a Visa for the country you are visiting.

Advance Preparation

- Book the car in for a service well in advance of the departure date. Tyres, fan belt, plugs, radiator and battery should be checked thoroughly
- Contact your insurers about a Green Card and any extra insurance you may require at least a month ahead of your travel date
- Get a spare car key cut
- Make sure you have sufficient maps, guidebooks, reference books to explore the country you are visiting to the fullest extent. Your local AA Centre will have a good range.

Motoring Holidays In The UK

Disabled people holidaying in the UK are in luck, because the SIA holds a wealth of information on accessible holiday accommodation, including self-catering establishments, hotels and guesthouses and adventure centres as well as details of wheelchair toilets all over the UK, and accessible places to visit. All of this information is only a phone call away.

The majority of motorway service stations in the UK have toilets which are accessible to disabled people, but the standard is variable. The other facilities (such as shops, restaurants, etc.) may not always be totally accessible. The AA ***Guide for the Disabled Traveller*** gives access details of all motorway service stations to help you plan rest stops on the journey.

On non-motorway routes, finding an accessible loo can be more difficult. The RADAR National Key Scheme for using accessible toilets is now widely used throughout the UK and it would be advisable to obtain one of these keys, which comes with a list of toilets in the scheme, from RADAR before travelling, otherwise you may find yourself locked out of the only wheelchair-accessible toilet within a radius of 100 miles. Those not familiar with the Key Scheme can obtain further details from RADAR.

For Orange Badge holders there are concessions on some toll bridges. These include the Severn, Erskine, Tay and Forth road bridges. Further details of concessions at toll bridges can be found in the AA ***Guide for the Disabled Traveller***.

As more and more petrol stations become self-service, it is increasingly difficult to fill up your tank unless you travel with an able-bodied companion. 'Help' pennants can be used to attract attention if you need assistance at the petrol pumps. There is also a booklet ***Easier Motoring for Disabled Drivers - a Directory of Facilities Available At Shell Garages*** which gives a run-down of accessible facilities across the UK.

Whether you are driving at home or abroad, it is a good idea to belong to one of the national breakdown associations.

The AA allows disabled drivers who drive Motability cars to join without paying the basic enrolment fee. The concession includes the 24-hour breakdown service. The RAC will give a reduced subscription to DDMC members, and the National Breakdown and Recovery Club operates a special reduced-price breakdown scheme for the disabled driver.

ROAD TRAVELLERS' DIRECTORY - USEFUL ADDRESSES

- **The Automobile Association (AA)**
  Fanum House
  Basingstoke
  Hants
  RG21 2EA
  Tel: (0256) 20123

- **Department of Transport**
  2 Marsham Street
  London SW1P 3EB
  Tel: 071-276 3000

- **Driver and Vehicle Licensing Centre (DVLC)**
  Swansea SA99 1AB
  (applications)

- **DVLC**
  Swansea SA6 7LJ
  (enquiries)

- **Royal Automobile Club (RAC)**
  RAC House
  7 Brighton Road
  Croydon CR2 6XW
  Tel: 081-686 2525

- **P & H Enterprises Ltd**
  PO Box No 59D
  New Malden
  Surrey KT3 5BR
  Tel: 081-942 9094

  Disposable Car Loo pack for men and women.

USEFUL PUBLICATIONS

- ***Motoring and Mobility for Disabled People***

  RADAR
  25 Mortimer Street
  London W1N 8AB
  Tel: 071-637 5400

- AA *Guide for the Disabled Traveller* (Free to members) and ***Hotels and Restaurants in Europe***

  Automobile Association
  Fanum House
  Basingstoke
  Hants RG21 2EA
  Tel: (0256) 20123

- ***DDMC Yearbook***

  Disabled Drivers Motor Club (DDMC)
  1a Dudley Gardens
  London W13 9LU
  Tel: 081-840 1515

MOTORING ACCESSORIES

- **Tony Mason Auto Products**
  Woodford House
  Great Central Way
  Near Daventry
  Northants NN1 6PZ
  Tel: (0237) 61771

  Emergency kit including a tyre inflator, set of booster cables, tow rope, warning triangle, 'on tow' sign and slip-over fluorescent jacket.

- **New Concept**
  PO Box 61
  Winchester
  Hants SO23 8XR
  Tel: (0962) 65996

  Easilift Airjack is inflated through tubing connected to the exhaust pipe but beware of vehicle instability when using it. Suitable for vehicles up to 2.25 tons.

CAR HIRE IN THE UK AND ABROAD

Wheelchair users flying to a holiday or business destination may find that renting a car adapted to hand-controls gives them more flexibility and freedom.

A number of car rental companies offer a service to disabled drivers. Terms and conditions such as age limit of driver, number of drivers allowed to use the car, type of licence required, pick-up and drop-off policies, mileage allowance - some car rental companies offer unlimited mileage, others do not - may vary from company to company. You will need a valid full drivers' licence and in some countries you may require an International Driving Permit. It will also be necessary to present some sort of credit identification to the car rental company, such as one of the major credit cards. If you intend to pay the final bill by credit card, find out which are acceptable to the company, and whether a cash deposit will be required for the vehicle and/or the hand-controls.

It is a good idea to contact your vehicle insurance company before you travel to see if any extra cover is required (apart from the Green Card for driving in Europe).

Avis and Hertz operate worldwide and have cars with hand-controls available for rent in most major cities throughout Canada and the USA. The rental car can usually be picked up and dropped off at the airport. However, in many European countries rental cars equipped with hand-controls are few and far between.

Car hire companies usually require at least three weeks advance notice for hand-controlled cars, and when booking you should specify whether you want a two or four-door car (most wheelchair users prefer two-door cars as they find it easier to transfer in to them from their wheelchair); the size and style of car, (eg one with a boot large enough to hold a folded wheelchair) and whether you want the hand-controls mounted on the right or left of the steering wheel. Some car rental companies will allow you to bring your own set of hand-controls with you and a mechanic will fit them to the car for an extra cost, but check this with the car rental company well in advance. Some companies will only allow hand-controlled cars to be dropped off at their original pick-up point, so check on pick-up and drop-off procedures. Also determine what sort of insurance and car documentation is required by them for you to rent and drive the car. Get confirmation of rental conditions and hand-control requirements in writing before you travel.

When you pick up your rental car, make sure you are familiar with the hand-controls, as in many countries they will operate in a different way to your own. Make sure the controls are in good working order and check the car over completely before you drive off so that you will not be held responsible for someone else's scrapes and bumps.

In the USA it is also possible to rent vans and travel homes fully equipped for either disabled drivers or passengers, which opens up a whole range of exciting possibilities for disabled travellers. The vehicles come equipped with wheelchair lifts and tie-downs, raised roofs and raised door openings. Hand-controls are available if required.

Some of the major rental companies who have hand-controlled cars available to rent are:

Australia *Budget Rent-a-Car*
21 Bedford Street
North Melbourne
Victoria

France *Inter-Touring Service*
117 Boulevard Auguste Blanqui
75013 Paris

UK *Hertz* Tel: 081-897 3347 has specially equipped cars for disabled drivers available throughout central London and at Heathrow and Gatwick Airports.

Hertz would like three days notice in order to arrange for a hand-controlled car to be available, for use in this country only. Optional insurance is extra.

Kenning Car Rental Tel: 081-882 3576 Kenning Car Hire offers a selection of hatchback and saloon cars with automatic transmission and hand-controls for self-drive hire.

W Harold Perry Ltd Tel: 081-951 5479 Perry's offers a selection of Ford cars at very favourable rates with automatic transmission and hand-controls for self-drive hire and, providing you have all the necessary insurance and documents, will allow youto travel with the car to Europe.

USA For further information on rates and details of specially equipped vans for hire in the USA, write to

Drive Master Corporation
16-1 Andrews Drive
West Paterson
New Jersey 07424

Associated Leasing Handicapable Vans
35W P Cliff Street
600 121st St Bursville
MN 55337

COACH STATIONS

It is now the policy to design new coach stations with wheelchair users in mind and some of the newer stations do have facilities such as accessible toilets and refreshment areas. However, many of the older ones have no wheelchair access so ask at your local coach station to find out what facilities are available.

COACHES

Coaches are not usually accessible to wheelchair users. However, National Express, who have a network of coach services in the UK, can provide assistance for disabled passengers at some of their terminals. At Victoria coach station, for example, some help is available, but always check in advance of your travel date so that arrangements can be made.

COACH HIRE FOR DISABLED PEOPLE

- **The Chalfont Line**
  4 Medway Parade
  Western Avenue
  Perivale
  Greenford
  Middlesex UB6 8HR
  Tel: 081-997 3799

This company operates minibuses which are fully adapted to carry disabled passengers, with tail lifts and removable seating. They also operate a fully adapted luxury coach with hydraulic life and removable seating.

- **Premier Travel Service Ltd**
  Premier Park
  King Hedges Road
  Cambs CB4 4PQ
  Tel: (0223) 237262

  This company operates three coaches equipped with hydraulic lifts for wheelchair users.

- **Millars Coaches**
  16/18 Cambridge Road
  Foxton
  Cambs CB2 6SH
  Tel: (0223) 870220

  Two coaches with hydraulic lifts for wheelchair users

- **National Express Coaches Ltd**
  172 Buckingham Palace Road
  London SW1W 9TN
  Tel: 071-730 0202

  Several companies within the National Express Coach Company have specially adapted vehicles for use by disabled people. These vehicles have been converted under stringent safety guidelines and many of the local companies who operate them can provide a full coach charter service which includes advice with itineraries, arranged tours, accommodation and overseas travel.

USEFUL PUBLICATIONS

A booklet ***Getting Around by Bus and Coach - A Guide for People with Disabilities*** gives details of operators with special vehicles for hire. Contact:

UK **Bus and Coach Council**
Sardinia House
52 Lincoln's Inn Fields
London WC2A 3LZ
Tel: 071-831 7546

USA **SATH** (Society for the Advancement of Travel for the Handicapped)
26 Court Street
Suite 100
Brooklyn
New York 11242

For information on all forms of travel in the USA. SATH also publishes a booklet ***The United States Welcomes Handicapped Visitors***.

Highway Rest Areas for Handicapped Travellers
President's Committee on Employment of the Handicapped
Washington DV 20010

New York State Thruway Facilities for the Handicapped
New York State Thruway Authority
Albany
New York 12201

· *CHAPTER NINE* ·

TRAVELLING BY SEA

CAR FERRIES

For those who prefer the adventure of a sea crossing and the open road to air travel and a package holiday, some guidelines are worth noting.

Taking the car abroad need not be as daunting as it sounds, provided you have planned well in advance and followed the advice in this book on essential documents you will need, and Continental motoring laws etc.

A motoring holiday abroad gives most disabled people, whether drivers or passengers, a degree of independence not possible on other types of foreign holiday. There is freedom to explore the countryside at your own pace with no schedules or timetables to stick to. Motoring on the Continent means you will have to travel by one of the cross-channel ferries, and when choosing the shipping company, bear the following points in mind. The channel port nearest to your home and your destination will be an important consideration, but other points to consider are - is there an adequate lift and a wheelchair-acccessible loo on board? Can you move around comfortably? Are the facilities you need available at terminals either end of your journey?

Also find out about flexibility of sailing times - the shorter crossings are most frequent and on the longer crossings there may be only one or two ships a day, so if you miss the boat you may have to wait a day or two until there is another sailing.

Generally speaking, on a pence-per-mile basis, the longer crossings are a much better buy than the shorter ones. The leading ferry companies have sliced up the channel routes between them, so prices tend to be much the same, but enormous savings can be made by travelling at off-peak times.

P & O European Ferries and Sealink are the biggest cross-channel ferry operators with the most routes. It is always worth checking which operators are offering off-peak inducements, concessions for disabled drivers, reductions for children, etc, for the best possible price. Among regular cross-channel travellers, the most popular way of cutting fares is by investing in P & O Ferries. Holders of preference shares in European Ferries are entitled to discounts of up to 50 per cent on certain crossings. Sealink offers an Auto Club promotion whereby members of the club return their ticket stubs and receive a voucher entitling them to 20 per cent off their next sea crossing. It is always worth keeping a lookout for promotions and perks offered by rival ferry companies.

Concessions offered to disabled drivers and passengers by the different shipping companies vary considerably, but most shipping companies on cross-channel routes offer disabled drivers whose cars have been adapted free or discounted passage for their vehicles. This applies to the vehicle only - passengers and drivers pay the going rate. Usually these concessions are given to fully paid up members of either the DDA or DDMC, but Sealink accept a verification from your Social Services Department. The DDA or DDMC will send a certificate of membership and special letter on your behalf to the shipping company if necessary. The historical reason for the concession being given to DDA and DDMC members is that originally the shipping companies gave the concession to drivers of three-wheeled trikes. With the phasing out of the trike the concession has remained in the hands of the DDA and DDMC to negotiate. The concession represents a considerable saving, find out more about it if you are not a DDA or DDMC member.

Both organisations charge an administration fee for processing each application. The DDA and the DDMC both publish useful leaflets which describe the application procedure and the names and addresses of operators granting concessions.

Advance warning

Most of the cross-channel ferry operators ask for prior notification of your proposed crossing time and other information such as the make, colour and registration number of your car, the number of your seat or cabin reservation (if appropriate), whether you are a wheelchair user and any assistance you may need, including lifting up stairs if adequate lifts are not available. You can telephone this information through to the company's booking office, but it is always wise to put it in writing and retain a copy of the letter.

If you are planning a night crossing, make sure you have a comfortable and accessible cabin where you can get a good night's sleep. An advantage of using the longer cross-channel routes is that they can sometimes shorten the drive at the other end and using the night ferry means that for at least one night you will not need to search for accessible hotel accommodation.

Information about accessible facilities offered by the different shipping companies may be hard to come by. Invariably, staff at the shipping company's Head Office will tell you that there are adequate facilities for disabled people and that it can cater for people in wheelchairs, but become vague when it comes to specific details. Travel on personal recommendation if you can, or failing that, make contact direct with the Port Office Manager of the shipping company with which you wish to travel, as he/she will have a better idea of the facilities available both on board and at the terminal. Some operators are more helpful than others but usually the newer and more modern ships run by the larger operators like Sealink tend to be better equipped than the smaller companies.

North Sea Ferries, the Sally Line, and the Olau Line, for instance, have excellent facilities for disabled passengers.

Procedure for boarding

Inform the shipping company of your disability and the help you are likely to need, both at the port and on board, when making your reservations. Most ferry companies ask disabled drivers to arrive an hour or more ahead of sailing time, so they can be placed at the front of the vehicle queue to board the ferry. If you arrive late at the car passenger terminal you may find that your access to the service lift is blocked by cars and lorries which have already been loaded on to the car deck. You will not need to get out of your car before driving on board but you will need to have your travel documents at the ready (passport, tickets, cabin reservations, and Green Card if required) so as not to create any delay at passport control. Tell the ferry staff immediately you arrive at the dock that you are a disabled traveller needing some assistance. They can then radio ahead to the Ferry Loading Officer to make sure someone is standing by to direct you to the right spot and give you further information. Many of the larger ferry companies identify disabled passengers by putting their own sticker on your windscreen - this helps the loading officer to spot your car and give you a prime parking place by the lift.

Shipping companies advise customers for safety reasons not to carry spare filled petrol containers or a full tank of petrol whilst on board ship.

Incidentally, if you are travelling on a ship that has no wheelchair-accessible toilet make sure to use those in the terminal building before departure. Wheelchair-accessible toilets at channel ports in the UK are listed at the end of this chapter. If you need to get out of your car to use the restaurant, telephone or Bureau de Change, it might be worth tracking down a copy of the publication ***Access at the Channel Ports*** which gives details of accessible buildings and facilities at all the ports, including those on the other side of the Channel.

Once on board, the ferry crew are usually very helpful and will offer assistance if required. However, do not allow yourself to be rushed - take your time getting out of your car and into your wheelchair and collecting your belongings so that you do not leave anything behind (there is no access to the car deck after sailing). On some ships there may be a large step into the lift, but ferry staff will either give you a helping hand or provide a ramp.

Not all service lifts are completely accessible and on some vessels footplates will have to be removed to enable a wheelchair to fit into the lift and the doors to close. On some ferries, where the lift is just a moving platform designed for deliveries it is advisable to tuck protruding feet well in! On some of the older ships the service lift may be too small to take a wheelchair. If this is the case you could improvise with a dining chair to sit on in the lift and your wheelchair can follow in a separate journey to the passenger deck where the chair-to-wheelchair transfer routine can be reversed. On older ships there may be no lift at all, but members of the ferry crew are usually willing to carry you and your wheelchair up the stairs. However, there is considerable advantage in finding out about facilities on board before travelling and choosing a route where there are fewer problems.

The passenger deck can become very crowded, especially during school holiday time and obviously at the peak of the summer season, so if you are taking a longer voyage it might be worthwhile booking yourself a cabin or reclining seat. Most of the shipping companies do have cabins which they allocate to disabled travellers. These may not necessarily be specially adapted but have flat access and are sited close to service lifts and you should be able to transfer on to a lower bunk. On some ships the toilets in these cabins have 4 inch risers at the threshold so access to use the toilet may not be possible without help. Find out if there is a wheelchair-accessible toilet on board, as some shipping companies assume you can use the toilet in your cabin. The two-berth cabins are very cramped for wheelchair users, so if you can afford it, a four berth cabin offers a bit more space alongside the bunks for transferring from wheelchair to bunk bed. On some of the newer ships, de-luxe cabins have been installed with single beds, *en suite* toilets and washbasins and are more like hotel rooms than traditional-style cabins. These are much more suitable for disabled travellers using wheelchairs, but obviously more expensive.

A reclining seat can be booked in advance for a few extra pounds and can provide a comfortable and quiet place to read or snooze during the crossing. It should be possible to transfer comfortably from your wheelchair to the seat but some disabled people may need a helping hand. Check when booking that you can reach the reclining seat area in a wheelchair and whether the lift is handy.

Alternatively, find a table in the lounge where you are not on a main thoroughfare to the bar or an exit door and liable to be bumped and jostled. These prime spots fill up quickly, so make it your first priority when you get on board if you have not booked a cabin or reclining seat.

If the crossing looks like being very rough, ask one of the crew to secure your chair to the fixed seating to avoid rolling out of control.

Most of the newer, more modern ships have flat access to most parts and there are wheelchair-accessible toilets on board. On some, the disabled toilet is on the cabin deck and you will need to take the lift down. If you are not a good sailor it can be difficult to use the toilet when the ship is rolling in heavy seas, so go as soon as you board and before you settle down on the passenger deck to enjoy the voyage.

SEASICKNESS

Preventing motion or seasickness can be a problem, but the risk can be minimised by following these few steps, irrespective of whether or not travel sickness remedies are used.

Remember that the combination of diesel fumes and the motion of the ship can be devastating! It will help if you stay on deck and maintain a good view of the horizon. The ship appears to roll more below decks and this makes you feel worse. Find a place to sit in roughly the centre of the ship (called 'amidships' in seaman's parlance) as it is more stable and less subject to vibration and movement in bad weather. Seasickness or motionsickness is more likely to occur on smaller ships such as cross-channel ferries as most larger ships these days are fitted with stabilisers, (although some of the newer cross-channel ferries do have them). Try to avoid the fatigue of overnight travel and get a good night's rest before you travel. Smoking may aggravate the condition. If you are prone to seasickness, lie down as soon as possible after you board and avoid moving your head from side to side. If you do feel queasy there is not much you can do apart from lying down, keeping still and sipping iced water slowly. If you plan to take seasickness pills to prevent *mal de mer* during the crossing, you must remember to take them an hour or so before you travel for them to work effectively. Also remember that some seasickness remedies have unwanted side effects such as drowsiness, so do not drive until any feelings of sleepiness have worn off. Dramamine and Quells are classic anti-nausea remedies or you could explore your local health food shop for a herbal preparation.

'Sea Bands'. The manufacturer of this novel idea claims it has a 98 per cent success rate with car sickness sufferers and 80 per cent with seasickness and they are so confident they work that they even offer a money back guarantee. The cloth bands are worn on the arm and work by putting pressure on one of the forearm's acupressure points. Because the treatment is drug free there are no nasty side effects. Sea Bands cost £6.50 from chemists, shipping companies or from the ships chandleries.

On the larger, more modern ships you will find everything you need on board; restaurants, self-service cafeterias, duty-free shop, Bureau de Change, etc. If all you will want during the voyage is a cup of coffee, it might be worth taking a thermos flask with you as the facilities do get very crowded, especially during the peak season, and trying to weave your way through throngs of people on a lurching ship in a wheelchair may prove a challenge.

ACCESS AT UK CHANNEL PORTS

Dover - Eastern Docks

Good access to buffet, shops, booking hall, and car waiting rooms. Wheelchair-accessible toilets in the booking hall, at No.6 berth, and in the restaurant complex (Barnacles) in the waiting area.

Car-parking facilities for severely disabled travellers are controlled by the Dover Harbour Board who will provide parking spaces subject to prior notice in writing.

Further information from:

- The Duty Traffic Controller
  Eastern Docks
  Dover
  Kent
  Tel: (0304) 240400

Dover - Western Docks

Wheelchair-accessible toilet on No.3 platform of the station, and in the railway buffet.

Short-term car parking is available if notice is given to Sealink Port Office. Tel: (0304) 203203

Further information from:

- Shipping Services Manager
  Southern House
  Dover
  Kent
  Tel: (0304) 203203

Dover Hoverport

Good general access with wheelchair-accessible toilet in the Departure Lounge.

Felixstowe Passenger Terminal

Good general access to all facilities with wheelchair-accessible toilet in the Passenger Terminal.

Short-term car parking is available in the terminal area, and access from the car park to the terminal is suitable for wheelchair users.

Further information from:

- European Operations Manager
  P & O European Ferries Ltd
  European House
  The Docks
  Felixstowe
  Suffolk IP11 8TB
  Tel: (0394) 604100

Folkestone Car Ferry Terminal

There are wheelchair-accessible toilets in the west side terminal and platform 1 nearest the terminal. Access to all other facilities is by outside walkways to departure lounges, customs and immigration controls. All at ground level. Buffet adjacent to Travel Centre is accessible to wheelchair users.

Short-term car parking is available upon request to the Port Manager.

Further information from:

- Sealink British Ferries
  Folkestone Harbour
  Folkestone
  Kent CT20 1QH
  Tel: (0303) 54947

Harwich (Parkeston Quay) Car Ferry Terminal

Buffet, Bureau de Change, AA and RAC Offices in Terminal Reception Area are all accessible to a wheelchair user, although there is a small step at the entrance. There is a disabled persons' toilet with fixed handrails. An improvement programme is planned to upgrade facilities at the port.

Further information from:

- The Port Manager
  Sealink UK Ltd.
  Parkeston Quay
  Harwich
  Essex CO12 4SR
  Tel: (0255) 242000
  or Sealink Travel Centre. Tel: (0255) 243333

Hull

North Sea Ferries has a new terminal building with wheelchair-accessible toilets on the ground and first floor. There is a lift and all facilities are accessible to disabled travellers. There is a short-term car park where cars may be left free of charge at owners' risk, adjacent to terminal building.

Further information from:

- The Sales and Passenger Manager
  North Sea Ferries Ltd.
  King George Dock
  Hedon Road
  Hull HV9 5GA
  Tel: (0482) 795141.

Newhaven - Sealink Car Ferry Terminal

Main door is about 5ft wide and is reached by two low steps of 4in height. Inside the terminal there is level access to buffet, AA office and Thomas Cook Exchange Bureau. There are no wheelchair-accessible toilets. Doors to ordinary cubicles are 2ft 2in wide. There is short-term parking to use terminal only.

Further information from:

- The Shipping and Port Manager
  Sealink UK Ltd.
  Newhaven Harbour
  Newhaven BN9 0BG
  Tel: (0273) 516699.

Plymouth - Brittany Ferries Terminal

There is a ramp for access to the terminal building, but no wheelchair-accessible toilet. Nearest accessible loo is at Derry's Cross.

Further information from:

- The Port and Shipping Manager
  Associated British Ports
  Port Office
  Millbay Docks
  Plymouth PL1 3EW
  Tel: (0752) 221321.

Portsmouth Passenger Terminal

Access to terminal is level and there is wheelchair access to Bureau de Change, shipping line offices, cafe and shop. Wheelchair-accessible toilets.

Further information from:

- The Port Manager
  Harbour Offices
  Continental Ferry Port
  George Byng Way
  Portsmouth PO2 8SP
  Tel: (0705) 834791
  or from Sealink Office. Tel: (0705) 811315.

Sheerness Passenger Terminal

Toilets for disabled people are located in the main passenger waiting area inside the terminal which is on the ground floor and all parts are accessible by wheelchair. There is a short-term car park available at the main entrance which is approximately 500 yards from the terminal.

Further information from:

- The Passenger Manager
  Olau Line UK Ltd.
  The Old Paymaster House
  104 Anchor Lane
  Sheerness Docks
  Kent ME12 1SN
  Tel: (0795) 666666

Southampton Passenger Terminal

Good general access, but no wheelchair-accessible toilet.

Weymouth Passenger Terminal

Good general access with wheelchair-accessible toilets.

Channel Island Ports

Guernsey

A small terminal with wheelchair-accessible unisex toilet available.

Further information from:

- The Harbourmaster
  White Rock
  St Peter Port
  Guernsey, CI.
  Tel: (0481) 20229

Jersey

Ramped access to passenger terminals with a unisex wheelchair-accessible toilet in Terminal 1.

Further information from:

- The Harbourmaster
  PO Box 599
  St Helier
  Jersey, CI

or

- Sealink Office
  76 Wests Centre
  Bath Street
  St Helier
  Tel: (0534) 34451.

Concessions Offered By Principal Cross-Channel Shipping Companies

Sealink UK Ltd

- Charter House
  Park Street
  Ashford
  Kent TN24 8TX
- **Cross-channel routes:**
  Harwich - Hoek Van Holland
  Dover - Calais
  Folkestone - Boulogne
  Newhaven - Dieppe
  Portsmouth/Weymouth - Cherbourg
- **Ireland:**
  Holyhead - Dun Laoghaire
  Fishguard - Rosslare
  Holyhead - Dublin
  Liverpool - Dublin
  Stranraer - Larne
- **Isle of Wight:**
  Portsmouth - Fishbourne
  Lymington - Yarmouth
- **Channel Islands:**
  Portsmouth - Guernsey/Jersey
  Weymouth - Jersey/Guernsey
- **Concessions:**
  Free conveyance of vehicle for disabled drivers is offered on the above routes, provided they are members of DDA or DDMC. If you are registered as a disabled person with your local authority, send for an application form from Sealink at the above address which will then need to be countersigned by your local Department of Social Services.

  Advance notice is necessary, and wharfage charge is payable to Sealink to cover harbour dues and administration.
- **Accessible facilities:**
  Sealink's older ships are not fully accessible to people in wheelchairs, but its newer ships the ***Flagship Service***; the ***St Anselm, St Christopher, The Champs Elyses***, and ***Cote d'Azur*** are fully adapted with large service lifts, wheelchair-accessible toilets and good general access.

P & O European Ferries PLC

- Channel House
  Channel View Road
  Dover, Kent CT18 9TJ
  Tel: (0304) 203388
- **Cross-channel routes:**
  Dover - Calais
  Dover - Boulogne
  Dover - Zeebrugge
  Dover - Ostende
  Felixstowe - Zeebrugge
  Portsmouth - Le Havre/Cherbourg
- **Ireland:**
  Cairnryan, Scotland - Larne, N Ireland
- **Concessions:**
  Free conveyance of vehicles for disabled drivers who are members of the DDA or DDMC. This concession is extended to those members living on the Continent.
- **Accessible facilities:**
  All ships have good general access for people in wheelchairs, including lifts from car deck to passenger deck and wheelchair-accessible toilets on all routes *except* the Dover-Ostende route. P & O asks for prior notice if you are disabled so it can have extra crew members standing by on the car deck to assist you to operate the service lift from the car to the passenger deck. Parking close to service lift available. Accessible cabins and couchettes on some routes.

  Excellent facilities for disabled travellers on P & O European Ferries *Blue Riband* ships operating between Dover and Calais.

Brittany Ferries

- Brittany Ferries Office
  Millbay Docks
  Plymouth PL1 3EW
  Tel: (0752) 221321
- **Cross-channel routes:**
  Portsmouth - St Malo
  Portsmouth - Caen
  Plymouth - Roscoff
  Plymouth - Santander (Spain)
- **Concessions:**
  Registered disabled drivers may take their vehicles free of charge on

cross-channel routes (with some restrictions on the Portsmouth to St Malo service).

- **Accessible facilities:**
Brittany Ferries advises that there are several cabins which have wide entrances specifically for wheelchair users and there is a lift between the car deck and the main accommodation deck. However, the cafeteria and duty free shops are on a higher deck which entails negotiating a steep flight of stairs. On the *Quiberion* there is a wheelchair-accessible toilet adjacent to the two-berth cabin allocated to disabled travellers, usually no.161. The toilet inside the cabin is inaccessible. The four-berth cabins along the same corridor are considerably more spacious for wheelchair users. On the *Duke of Normandy* cabin no.301 is offered to disabled travellers as it has flat access but the space is very cramped and there is a 4in threshold dividing the cabin and the toilet. There is no disabled toilet on the *Duke of Normandy*.

The *Bretagne* has some facilities for wheelchair travellers.

The advantage of travelling Brittany Ferries routes is that they often cut out a great deal of the driving at the other end and also provide a bed on the night sailings. If you wish to book a cabin suitable for disabled travellers, do so well in advance.

North Sea Ferries Ltd

- King George Dock
Hedon Road
Hull
North Humberside HU9 5GA
Tel: (0482) 77177
- **Cross-channel routes:**
Hull - Rotterdam/Zeebrugge
- **Concessions:**
Free conveyance of vehicle for disabled drivers who are DDA or DDMC members, or members of the International Aid for the Disabled Travellers Club.
- **Accessible facilities:**
Vessels *Norwind* and *Norstar* have lifts serving all decks (approximate dimensions: door 3ft, width 4ft, depth 5ft) and two 2-berth cabins with wider doors and toilet facilities for wheelchair users.

Some vessels on some routes are not suitable for disabled passengers, so make sure you are booked on a vessel which meets your requirements.

Arrangements can be made to park your car near a service lift.

North Sea Ferries says its terminal building has good access, with wheelchair-accessible toilets.

Olau Line (UK) Ltd

- Sheerness
104 Anchor Lane
Sheerness
Kent MT12 15N
Tel: (0795) 580010
- **Cross-channel routes:**
Sheerness - Vlissinger, Holland
- **Concessions:**
Free conveyance of vehicle for disabled drivers who are DDA or DDMA members.
- **Accessible facilities:**
All ships have passenger and service lifts between decks. There are two adapted cabins for wheelchair passengers with accessible toilet and shower.
Arrangements can be made to park the car close to the lift which is large enough to take a wheelchair and passenger.
Terminal building is completely accessible.

Sally Line

- Argyle Centre
York Street
Ramsgate
Kent CT11 9DS
Tel: (0843) 595522
- **Cross-channel routes:**
Ramsgate - Dunkirk
- **Concessions:**
No concessions or discounts available to disabled drivers.
- **Accessible facilities:**
There are lifts on board and wheelchair-accessible toilets.

Ramsgate and Dunkirk terminals have good access and wheelchair-accessible toilets.

DFDS Seaways

- Scandanavia House
  Parkeston Quay
  Harwich
  Essex CO12 4QG
  Tel: (0255) 240240
- **Routes:**
  Harwich - Gothenburg, Sweden
  Newcastle - Gothenburg
  Harwich - Esbjerg, Denmark
  Newcastle - Esbjerg
  Harwich - Hamburg, Germany
- **Concessions:**
  Free conveyance of vehicle for disabled drivers who are members of the DDA, DDMC or Travellers Club.
- **Accessible facilities:**
  General access on board ship is good and there are accessible lifts from car deck to passenger decks which can accommodate wheelchairs.

  DFDS vessels *Dan Anglia, Tor Brittania* and *Tor Scandinavia* have special cabins designed for disabled people which include wheelchair-accessible private bathroom.

B & I Line

- Reliance House
  Water Street
  Liverpool L2 8TP
  Tel: 051-227 3131
- **Routes:**
  Liverpool - Dublin, Ireland
  Holyhead - Dublin
  Fishguard - Rosslare, Ireland
- **Concessions:**
  Free conveyance of vehicle provided for members of the DDA or DDMC. The concession is available all year except between 2 July - 5 September, Friday, Saturday, Sunday and Monday.

  B & I offers a concession of one-third off the ordinary single fare to holders of the Disabled Persons Railcard.
- **Accessible facilities:**
  Advance notification is required to park close to the lift. Accessible service lift available from car to passenger deck. Cabins with toilet facilities and extra wide doors are available but as they are limited should be booked well in advance.

  General access on board is good. Terminal has good general access.

Norway Line Ltd

- Tine Commission Quay
  Albert Edward Dock
  North Shields
  Tyne & Wear
  NE29 6EA
  Tel: 091-298 1313
- **Routes:**
  Newcastle - Stavanger, Bergen, Norway.
- **Concessions:**
  Free conveyance of vehicle provided for members of the DDA or DDMC.

P & O European Ferries

- Peninsular House
  Portsmouth
  PO2 8TA
  Tel: (0703) 772000
- **Routes:**
  Dover - Boulogne, Southampton - Le Havre
- **Concessions:**
  Free conveyance of vehicle for disabled drivers who are members of the DDA or DDMC.
- **Accessible facilities:**
  All ships have a service lift and some, not all, have wheelchair-accessible toilets.

Fred Olsen Line

- Crown House
  Crown Street
  Ipswich
  Suffolk IP1 3HB
  Tel: (0473) 233022
- **Routes:**
  Harwich - Oslo
- **Concessions:**
  Fred Olsen gives a 50 per cent reduction on passenger fares only (not vehicle)

subject to certification and only during out-of-season sailings.

- **Accessible facilities:**
  There is a lift from the car deck to passenger decks which can carry a wheelchair and there are also adequate lifts to all decks. Some cabins are specially fitted for disabled passengers - they are large and have flat access.

Hovercraft Services

- Hoverspeed
  Dover International Hoverport
  Kent CT17 9TG
  Tel: (0304) 240241 (reservations)

  There are no concessions for disabled travellers. Contact the Duty Officer (0304) 240101 ext 2235 to make any special travel arrangements.

- **Accessible facilities:**
  General access at the terminal building is good, with a special unisex toilet in the Departure Lounge. On the SRN4 hovercraft there are five steps between the car deck and passenger deck but, with prior notice, passengers in wheelchairs can be given assistance up the steps. Disabled travellers are required to transfer into a seat from their wheelchair, but permission may be given to remain in the car, provided they are accompanied. There are no wheelchair-accessible toilets on board.

  Crossings on the hovercraft take only 35 minutes, but can be rough!

ACCESS AT CONTINENTAL PORTS

FRANCE

Boulogne

There are toilets and a buffet at the terminal which are accessible to wheelchair users. Car parking could be arranged on advance application to the Boulogne Chamber of Commerce or the Ferry Operators.

Boulogne Hoverport

The terminal is flat throughout and there are wheelchair- accessible toilets.

Caen

A small port with flat access to all facilities.

Calais

There are toilets, buffet and restaurant (accessible by wide lifts) available to people in wheelchairs.

Car parking is the province of the port authority (the Calais Chamber of Commerce), who can make special arrangements provided it receives advance notice.

Calais Hoverport

Two steps to terminal building but flat throughout inside. No wheelchair-accessible toilets.

Cherbourg

The entrance to the passenger terminal is ramped and there is flat access throughout. No wheelchair-adapted toilet.

Dieppe

The terminal is not very accessible with two steps to entrance and no wheelchair-accessible toilet.

Le Havre

Flat access at entrance and throughout. No wheelchair-accessible toilet.

Roscoff

Fairly good access with a wheelchair-accessible toilet in passenger terminal.

St Malo

A modern passenger terminal which has level access to all facilities, including shipping line offices, telephone, café, and wheelchair-accessible toilet. There is a disabled person's parking place sited close to the terminal entrance.

HOLLAND

Hoek Van Holland

Four steps to passenger terminal entrance. No wheelchair-accessible toilets.

Ostend

Fairly good access throughout passenger terminal. There is a wheelchair-accessible toilet in the Jetfoil terminal lounge adjacent to the ferry terminal.

Rotterdam

Flat access throughout passenger terminal with wheelchair-accessible toilet.

Vlissingen (Flushing)

Two steps to passenger terminal entrance but flat access to all facilities inside and a wheelchair-adapted toilet.

BELGIUM

Zeebrugge

Both the P & O European Ferries Terminal and the North Sea Ferries Terminal are wheelchair-accessible. P & O has two handicapped car parking spaces adjacent to passenger terminal entrance.

SPAIN

Santander

Steps to terminal building but flat throughout inside. There is no wheelchair-accessible toilet.

For Further Information

The publication ***Access at the Channel Ports*** gives more detailed information on access and facilities at all the channel ports, both on this side of the channel and the other.

LOCAL FERRY SERVICES

The smaller ferries, such as those to the Scottish Islands, are part of the local transport system and as such do not always cater well for disabled travellers. On short crossings on open deck ferries, disabled travellers can stay in their cars, but on longer crossings on ferries with closed car decks this may not be possible. The majority of these ferries are fairly old and small and, therefore, are not equipped with lifts, ramps or toilets adapted for wheelchair users. If you need help you should contact the ferry operator to make any necessary arrangements. However, many of the ferry companies do give disabled drivers generous discounts and concessions.

FERRY COMPANIES WHO OFFER DISCOUNTS AND CONCESSIONS

P & O Scottish Ferries Ltd

- PO Box 5
  Jamieson Quay
  Aberdeen AB9 8DL
  Tel: (0224) 589 111
- **Routes:**
  Scrabster - Stromness
  Aberdeen - Lerwick
- **Concessions:**
  50 per cent discount for vehicle of disabled drivers belonging to DDA or DDMC. Wharfage charge added.

Belfast Car Ferry

- 47 Donegal Quay
  Belfast
  N Ireland
  Tel: (0232) 326800
- **Concessions:**
  50 per cent discount for vehicle and 50 per cent discount for driver belonging to DDA or DDMC.

Torbay Seaways

- 5 Beacon Quay
  Torbay
  Devon
  Tel: (0803) 214397
- **Routes:**
  Torbay - Channel Islands

Caledonian MacBrayne Ltd

- Ferry Terminal
  Gourock PA19 1GP
  Renfrewshire
  Tel: (0475) 33755
- **Routes:**
  The Clyde, Western Isles, Islay, Mull, Oban, Sky and Outer Isles.
- **Concessions:**
  50 per cent off vehicle for DDA/DDMC members.

Red Funnel Group

- 12 Bugle Street
  Southampton SO9 4LJ
  Tel: (0703) 333042
- **Routes:**
  Southampton - Cowes, Isle of Wight
- **Concessions:**
  50 per cent discount on vehicle for DDA/DDMC members

Harrison Clyde Ltd

- 16 Woodside Crescent
  Glasgow G3 7UT
  Tel: 041-332 9766
- **Routes:**
  Islay - Jura, Gourock - Dunoon
- **Concessions:**
  Discount on vehicles of DDA/DDMC members.

Isle of Man Seaways

- Sea Terminal
  Heysham
  Lancashire LA3 2XF
  Tel: (0524) 53802 (passenger services)
  (0524) 55052 (24-hour brochure service)
- **Routes:**
  Heysham - Douglas, Isle of Man
  From May - September:
  Fleetwood - Douglas
  Dublin - Douglas
  Belfast - Douglas
- **Concessions:**
  Vehicle 50 per cent discount if owned by driver and specially adapted.

British Channel Island Ferries

- Norman House
  Albert Johnson Quay
  Portsmouth
  Tel: (0202) 681155 (reservations)
- **Routes:**
  Poole - Jersey/Guernsey
- **Concessions:**
  Vehicles of disabled drivers free

USEFUL ADDRESSES

- Disabled Drivers Association (DDA)
  Ashwellthorpe
  Norwich NR16 1EX
  Tel: (0508) 41449
- Disabled Drivers Motor Club (DDMC)
  Cottingham Way
  Thrapston
  Northants NN14 4PL
  Tel: (08012) 4724
  Both organisations arrange concessions and issue leaflets which describe procedure for members to follow.

USEFUL PUBLICATIONS

- ***Access at the Channel Ports***
  Pauline Hephaistos Projects
  39 Bradley Gardens
  West Ealing
  London W1
- ***Holidays and Travel Abroad - A Guide for Disabled People***
  RADAR
  25 Mortimer Street
  London W1N 8AB
  Tel: 071-637 5400

CRUISING

Those who dream of treating themselves to a unique travel experience could do no better than to indulge in one of life's great holiday adventures - a luxury cruise. The cruise ships are like floating holiday hotels and offer the same luxuries and amenities that you would expect to find in a 5 star hotel anywhere in the world.

The first obstacle to overcome is convincing the shipping line that a wheelchair user can participate in and enjoy a cruising holiday without having to spend the entire voyage in the ship's hospital or accompanied by a full-time nurse! Most shipping companies have experience of elderly people or those with disabilities such as arthritis or heart complaints, who are able to stand and walk short distances when necessary and just need a transit wheelchair (not self-propelling) to get from one place to another on board ship. Some gentle persuasion is required to convince the shipping lines that paraplegics and tetraplegics who use wheelchairs permanently are just as fit and eager to try out their sea legs as the next passenger.

Although most ships are generally equipped with the same basic features and facilities, the design of each ship will vary considerably, so it is best to investigate which one suits your needs best. Cruising can present some architectural barriers to passengers in wheelchairs and it is important to find out as much as you can about the layout of the ship before you travel. Ask the shipping company you have chosen to supply you with a deck plan; from this you can get a good idea of which cabins will best suit a wheelchair-user. The plan will give positions of bunks, washbasin, wardrobes, etc. Once you have selected several cabins which may be a possibility, make a final decision when you view the ship to save time for both you and the shipping company. Write and ask the shipping line to clarify any points you may be unclear on, or ask your travel agent to do it for you. Keep all written confirmations safely and take copies with you when you travel.

For example, you may like to ask the following questions:

- Are there any particular cabins that are designed or more suitable for wheelchair users? If so, where are they located?
- Do any walls (or 'bulkheads', as they are called in seafaring parlance) have restrictive risers (usually about three or four inches) at doorways, leading to cabins and bathrooms recommended to disabled people?
- What are the width of cabin and lavatory doorways of the recommended cabin and does the bathroom door open inwards and block the lavatory when open? What are the dimensions of bathroom space? (Bathrooms are often small with narrow doorways and minimal turning space inside).
- What are the dimensions of cabin and bathroom doorways? (They may be very narrow).
- Is the passageway wide enough for turning your wheelchair into your cabin?
- Are passenger lifts on the ship large enough to take a wheelchair, and do they provide access to all decks? Ask for dimensions of lifts and which areas, if any, are not accessible.
- Are the entrances to restaurants, bars, entertainment lounges, cinemas and other public areas barrier-free?
- Where are the steps? Portable ramps may be provided by the company or, if necessary, bring your own.
- Is it possible to move any furniture which is blocking access into the cabin or is in excess of requirements, to enable freedom of movement?
- What height is the bed? If too low, request an extra mattress to bring it up to a comfortable height for transferring from wheelchair to bed, or bring your own set of bed blocks.
- If you want to bring your own motorised wheelchair, ask the shipping company if it will allow you to bring one on board. Some companies who operate cruise holidays do not allow them and also at some island ports motorised wheelchairs cannot be used without a permit. So be prepared to use your own collapsible manual chair while on holiday.
- What is the procedure for embarkation and debarkation?

Some people go straight to the top and write to the Managing Director of the shipping company they plan to cruise with, requesting a personal tour of the ship and the facilities at least six months in advance of the sailing date, after carefully studying the deck plan and selecting cabins which may be suitable for a wheelchair user. By this method you can choose a suitable cabin in the right price range.

Viewing the cabin of your choice is very important as you will be able to ascertain if furniture in the cabin can be re-arranged to allow a wheelchair user a clear passage. At the same time, choose a table in the dining room where a wheelchair will not cause obstruction. Also take a good look at the public rooms and open decks and decide whereabouts you would like ramps. Ramps are especially useful from amidships to the open decks as there are rather large bulkheads to overcome. The shipping line will arrange to have these made for you prior to sailing.

All in all, a day spent in Southampton looking over the ship could prove invaluable. It is no good cruising the Antipodes for six weeks if you cannot move around comfortably and join in the fun.

Usually cruise ships have three to eight decks. The upper deck is generally used for sunbathing and deck games, while the middle 'promenade' deck holds all the public rooms; bars, lounges, shops, cinema and outdoor pool. Below the promenade deck are the passenger cabins. Cabins described as being 'outside' have a porthole, or window, and those described as 'inside' have no portholes and are definitely not for the claustrophobic. Some cabins are equipped with *en suite* bathrooms with washbasin, toilet, shower or bath and passengers in wheelchairs need to make sure, either by personal inspection or written enquiry, that they are allocated a cabin where manoeuvrability is feasible and the adjoining toilet completely accessible. Naturally cabins with extra facilities, such as *en suite* bathroom or porthole cost more than those with shared facilities. If you find that as a wheelchair user you cannot get into the toilets in the cabin of your choice the best remedy is to ask the shipping line for a commode, or bring your own, rather than trying to use the public toilets around the ship.

There is usually a great deal of activity during the day to keep passengers occupied. Check that you can join in with this unless you are happy to relax with a good book and sunbathe. During the evening there will be entertainment and mealtimes on board ship are usually fairly long, drawn-out affairs with a huge variety of food on offer. Special diets, for diabetics or vegetarians, can be catered for if you make this known at the time of booking your holiday.

Do not book yourself on the shore excursions arranged by the shipping line, because the coaches will probably be unsuitable for a wheelchair user, besides which they are very expensive. If you can afford it, hire a taxi instead at the port of call and travel in comfort.

Your local travel agent should be able to tell you which shipping companies operate cruise holidays with suitable facilities for disabled passengers, or you can contact the cruise shipping companies direct. Brief instructions on the policy of the company towards accepting bookings from wheelchair passengers can usually be found in the brochure, but for more detailed and specific advice on accommodation and facilities a personal visit is recommended.

Details of shipping companies who operate cruise holidays with some facilities for disabled passengers follow. They are not completely barrier-free but have been reported to be more suitable than others, so it is vital you check the details thoroughly yourself.

P & O does have some facilities for passengers using wheelchairs on its *Island Princess* and *Royal Princess* cruiseliners. Passengers in wheelchairs can be booked into selected cabins thought suitable for their use, though cabins have not been specially adapted and none of the bathrooms within the cabins can accommodate a wheelchair because of the narrowness of the door and the raised threshold. However, there are specially adapted bathrooms located as near as possible to the cabins. On the *Star Princess*, P & O's most modern ship, there are specially designed cabins with wheelchair-accessible toilets and showers.

There are passenger lifts to most parts of the open decks and there is no problem with access to public rooms.

P & O has a battery-operated piece of equipment called an 'invalid crawler' to help disabled passengers embark and disembark. It can crawl up and down a gangway on caterpillar tracks and is operated by a crew member. The invalid crawler can carry any type of wheelchair provided it is not motorised.

Cunard advise that on its cruise ship *Queen Elizabeth II*, passengers in wheelchairs can be allocated suitable cabins with accessible *en suite* bathrooms. However, these fall into the most expensive price band. Assistance is available to help you embark and disembark.

Both P & O and Cunard request that passengers in wheelchairs are accompanied by an able-bodied companion. Some cruise lines ask disabled passengers to complete a medical certificate saying they are fit to travel. Disabled people often resent having to obtain medical clearance for taking part in normal activities, but shipping companies, like airlines, need to know whether medical or nursing care is required. If, for example, injections need to be given, they will need back-up medical notes and information on your condition from your doctor. They also need to know whether any assistance is required with daily rituals such as eating and using the toilet as cruise personnel cannot be responsible for providing personal care. If you need this type of care you will have to bring your own helper.

Ships cannot always dock in harbours, and difficulties arise if the cruise ship anchors at smaller ports where it is necessary to ferry passengers in tenders or motor launches to the shore. Both P & O and Cunard say that for safety reasons passengers in wheelchairs are not permitted to go ashore at anchor ports because of the potential dangers of getting disabled passengers from ship to tender, which often involves negotiating a flight of stairs or climbing down a ladder to reach the launch. In some cases, the crew will carry wheelchair passengers to and from the launch, but this service is not always provided. P & O has some excursion launches which can be loaded at deck level.

You may, of course, be quite content to remain on board while the other passengers explore the smaller ports - a full service is offered to those who choose to remain on ship. However, it is possible to plan your cruise programme so that you do not call at the smaller ports where a tender is used to transport you to the shore.

It may also be worth remembering that generally no wheelchair-accessible transportation is available at port stops for excursion trips. This means relying on local taxis or plain pushing power - your own or your companion's.

Stringent safety precautions and some of the features necessary in cruising vessels,

such as high weather strips at cabin entrances may preclude wheelchair users from using all the facilities on board ship but there are plenty of amenities you can take advantage of, for example; the gourmet cuisine, nightly entertainment and relaxation.

Fred Olsen Line's ship *Black Prince*, which cruises around the Mediterranean, has two cabins which are specially fitted for disabled passengers; there are no steps into the cabins and the doors are wide enough to take a wheelchair. The toilet has grab rails and other facilities for disabled passengers.

Fred Olsen says that the only possible problem would be when taking shore excursions, since there is a ladder going from one of the decks down to the pontoon from where the shore excursion boats leave. However, the crew are willing to carry disabled passengers wishing to take the shore excursions down to the launch and their wheelchair can be taken on board.

All Scandinavian Seaways' overnight ferries have wheelchair-accessible cabins with *en-suite* toilets. The *Tor Scandinavia* and the *Dana Anglia* have specially adapted cabins and the cruise ship the *Winston Churchill* has a large cabin with a wheelchair-accessible bathroom.

Once on board, make sure your wheelchair is in good working order, especially the brakes, and always keep them on when you are not moving. As a safety precaution place wooden blocks or wedges under your wheels if the going gets rough. Tetraplegics may consider wearing a safety strap as well in rough weather.

Always make sure any special requests have been passed on to the crew by meeting with the purser as soon as you can.

Do not let seasickness spoil your cruise. If you feel seasick while on board, remember that most cruise ships have a well-equipped medical staff who can administer an anti-seasick injection.

Remember also to take all necessary medical supplies with you on the voyage and, most important, do not forget your wheelchair narrower and a bicycle pump in case of flat tyres. A bicycle pump may be the only thing your cruiseliner has not got on board!

Shipping companies with some accessible features for disabled passengers

- P & O Princess Voyages
  77 New Oxford Street
  London WC1A 1PP
  Tel: 071-831 1881
- Cunard
  South Western House
  Canute Road
  Southampton SO9 1ZA
  Tel: (0703) 229933
- Scandinavian Seaways
  15 Hanover Street
  London W1R 9HG
  Tel: 071-493 6696
- Fred Olsen Line
  Crown House
  Crown Street
  Ipswich
  Suffolk IP1 3HB
  Tel: (0473) 233022

CHAPTER TEN

TRAVEL TIPS AND USEFUL INFORMATION

BEFORE YOU GO: LAST-MINUTE REMINDERS

Pack outfits that can be worn in layers - easy to put on or take off according to the weather.

Remember to pack plenty of film for the camera or buy it duty free at the airport or on the ferry - in some countries it can be expensive. Take two purses away with you - one for English and one for foreign money.

Pack an extra fold-away shopping bag if you plan to visit the hypermarkets or bring home lots of souvenirs.

Remember to pack a phrase book, pocket dictionary or take ***The International Disabled Traveller's Phrase Book*** to help you choose a meal or cope with an emergency.

Take a spare pair of spectacles abroad with you plus your optical prescription just in case you break or lose a pair - they are surprisingly popular with thieves abroad. In some countries, like Cyprus, spectacles can be cheaper than at home.

Medication

When travelling with liquid medicine carry it in a small waterproof sponge bag to prevent spills.

If you are flying, all medication should be carried on board with you in case your bags are lost.

Always carry your prescription with you, preferably with duplicates in the language of the country you are visiting. Use the chemical (generic) name, not the brand name.

Remember to take a spare bed pan or urinal for emergency use. A full list of equipment can be obtained from the Disabled Living Foundation.

Emergency precautions

If you are travelling abroad for the first time you may feel happier carrying a card giving your name, nationality, language spoken, disability and level of lesion, type of medicine and tablets taken with their dosage, any allergy to treatments, eg penicillin, and the telephone number or address of a family member or friend who

can be contacted in case of emergency. These simple precautions will enable immediate help to be given.

Medic-Alert

Medic-Alert provides a service for those with medical problems which could be made worse by treatment after an accident or illness when the patient is unable to make known his or her particular condition and the best way to treat it. Members wear a metal emblem engraved on one side with the name Medic-Alert, and the phone number of the emergency service on the reverse side where the immediate medical problems of the wearer are also noted. Additional medical information is filed at the Emergency Headquarters where the telephone is manned 24 hours a day.

- The Medic-Alert Foundation
  17 Bridge Wharf
  156 Caledonian Road
  London N1 9UU
  Tel: 071-833 3034

Repair kit for your wheelchair

If you travel to foreign parts, remember that you will probably be doing a lot more pushing, perhaps over rough and uneven ground. Bumping over uneven roads or cobblestones abroad can be lethal on bottoms and wheelchairs. In case of a wheelchair breakdown, remember to take a spare inner tube, puncture repair kit, pump tyre levers, screw driver, spanner, pliers, small oil can, etc, or have solid tyres fitted, as not all roads abroad are surfaced. A spare set of wheelchair castors is a good idea.

PHONING HOME FROM ABROAD

A few years ago, finding wheelchair-accessible call boxes in Europe was akin to searching for the Holy Grail. Today, especially in France and Spain, modern call boxes seem to be everywhere, even in the most remote and unexpected places.

It is possible to make a telephone call home through the reception desk at your hotel, or if you are not actually staying in hotel accommodation, through any large hotel in the area, but as this will incur extra charges it is sensible to use a call box, if you can find one which is wheelchair-accessible, can figure out how to operate it and have plenty of coins handy. Several countries have cheaper international calls at certain times, so it is always worth making your call during the cheap rate time. Reverse charge or British Telecom chargecard calls are available through the International Operator.

In many countries it is now easy for you to dial Britain direct and make your own calls to the UK from public telephone boxes, providing you know the code for international direct dialling. It helps to write down the complete number before you start. This is always made up of the international access code, the country code for the UK (44), the UK area code which is the STD code or prefix, (remember to leave out the first 0) and finally the local number. For example, if you were phoning the SIA (telephone number 081-444 2121) from France you would dial 19 44 81 444 2121.

The dialling tone will probably be different from the one you are used to, but always make sure there is a tone before you start dialling (you may not hear it until you have inserted some coins) and that it stops once you begin. Insert the coins carefully, giving each one time to drop before inserting another. In some countries you dial a number which connects you with the international system and then wait for a second tone before you begin dialling the code for the UK. In other countries you can dial the code for international calls and then proceed to dial the whole number without pause. It can take up to a minute to wait for connection, during which time you may hear some unfamiliar tones. Any persistent tone or recorded announcement will mean your call has failed, so try again, otherwise you should hear the familiar UK ringing tone.

If you know you will want to use the phone abroad and are still unsure of the pro-

cedure for the country you will be visiting, British Telecom International issues a leaflet ***Don't Forget the Phone*** which tells you what digits to dial and what coins you will need when in Austria, Belgium, Cyprus, Denmark, Finland, France, West Germany, Greece, Israel, Italy, Luxembourg, Malta, Morocco, Netherlands, Norway Portugal, Spain, Sweden, Switzerland, Tunisia and Yugoslavia. For additional information call British Telecom free on (0800)272 172.

TROUBLE ABROAD - CONSULTING THE CONSUL

Most of the time all goes well for travellers abroad but occasionally things do go wrong. If you get into real difficulties you can usually turn to the British Consul. For example, loss of money, passport or anything else while abroad on holiday should first be reported to the local police who should issue a statement about the loss. If you still need help, contact the Consulate.

In the case of a fatal accident get in touch with the Consulate at once as they will know what special arrangements must be made.

It is a good idea to jot down the address and telephone number of the local British Embassy, High Commission or Consulate as soon as you arrive - and hope you will never need to use it. Your hotel or tour operator should be able to give you this information, or you can look it up in the local telephone directory. Most British Consulates operate an answerphone service giving details of office hours and an emergency telephone number. Here is what a Consul can and cannot do. A Consul can issue emergency passports, contact relatives or friends and ask them to help you with money or tickets, advise on how to transfer funds, provide a list of local lawyers, interpreters and doctors, arrange for the next of kin to be informed of an accident or a death and advise on procedures. A Consul cannot pay your hotel, medical or any other bills, pay for travel tickets, undertake work usually done by travel agents, airlines, banks or motoring organisations, get preferential treatment for you in hospital, give legal advice, investigate a crime, obtain work or a work permit for you.

If you want to know more about the British Consul abroad, a leaflet ***Consular Assistance Abroad*** is available from travel agents.

ACCOMMODATION FOR DISABLED TRAVELLERS

- **Thomsons Holidays**
  Greater London House
  Hampstead Road
  London NW1 7SD
  Tel: 071-387 9321
  (Client Welfare Department can deal with individual enquiries from disabled people)

- **Horizon Holidays/Wings Holidays**
  Broadway
  Edgbaston Fiveways
  Birmingham B15 1BB
  Tel: 021-632 6282
- **Sovereign Holidays/British Airways**
  Holidays
  Ground Star House
  London Road
  Crawley
  West Sussex
  Tel: (0293) 560777
- **Cosmos Holidays**
  17 Holmesdale Road
  Bromley
  Kent BR2 9LX
  Tel: 081-464 3444
- **Thomas Cook Holidays**
  PO Box 36
  Thrope Wood
  Peterborough PE1 1NH
  Tel: (0733) 63200 (Holiday Information Centre)
  or (0733) 555225 (provides telephone booking service and gives advice to disabled people)
- **Eurocamp**
  Edmundson House
  Tatton Street
  Knutsford
  Cheshire WA16 6BG
  Tel: (0565) 3844
  or 071-935 0628
- **Gold Star Holidays**
  Ryedale Building
  60 Piccadilly
  York YO1 1YX
  Tel: (0904) 628992
- **Meon Villas Holidays**
  Meon House
  College Street
  Petersfield
  Hants GU32 3JN
  Tel: (0703) 68411
- **Vacances Franco - Britanniques**
  Normandy House
  High Street
  Cheltenham
  Glos GL50 3HW
  Tel: (0242) 526338

The Holiday Care Service and the RADAR Guide give a more comprehensive list of tour operators who can cater to some extent for disabled people but their personal experience of dealing with wheelchair users may be limited. Always double-check that the holiday offer is all you are looking for.

- **Holiday Care Service**
  2 Old Bank Chambers
  Station Road
  Horley
  Surrey RH6 9HW
  Tel: (0293) 774535
- ***Holiday and Travel Abroad - A Guide for Disabled People***
  RADAR
  25 Mortimer Street
  London W1N 8AB
  Tel: 071-637 5400

Commercial companies who have some accommodation for disabled people

- **Blakes Holidays**
  Wroxham
  Norwich NR12 8DH
  Tel: (0603) 782911
- **Butlins Holiday Centres**
  Bognor Regis
  Sussex PO21 1JJ
  Tel: (0243) 820202
- **Pontins Holiday Camps**
  PO Box 100
  Saga House
  The Green
  Eccleston
  Chorley
  Lancs PR7 5QQ
  Tel: (0257) 452452
- **Country Farm Holidays**
  Shaw Mews
  Shaw Street
  Worcester WR1 3QQ
  Tel: (0905) 613744 - Ansaphone
  (0706) 830830 - Brochure Enquiries
  (0905) 613746 - Information

- **Country Holidays**
  Spring Mill
  Earby
  Colne
  Lancs BB8 6RN
  Tel: (0282) 445566
- Selection of properties throughout the UK catering for disabled people.
  Disabled Person's Helpline
  Tel: (0282) 445340
- **Home Share Holidays**
  3 Main Street
  Elgin
  Moray IV30 3BQ
  Tel: (0343) 48118 - Holiday Exchange

Hotels offering 'mini-break' holidays

- **Best Western Hotels**
  Vine House
  143 London Road
  Kingston upon Thames
  Surrey KT2 6NA
  Tel: 081-541 0050 (admin)
  081-541 0033 (reservations)
- **Crest Hotels Ltd**
  Bridge Street
  Banbury
  Oxon OX16 8RQ
  Tel: (02952) 67153
- **Holiday Inns International**
  10-12 New College Parade
  Finchley Road
  London NW3 5EP
  Tel: 071-722 7755
- **Marriott Hotels**
  80 Regent Street
  London W1R 6AQ
  Tel: 071-439 0281/071-434 2299
- **Ramada Hotel Group**
  160 Brompton Road
  London SW3 1HF
  Tel: 071-235 5264 or freephone 2146
- **Sheraton Hotels**
  The Kiln House
  210 New Kings Road
  London SW6 4NZ
  Tel: (0800) 353535 (freephone)
  or 071-731 5857
- **Little Chef Lodge**
  Trusthouse Forte (UK) Ltd
  24-30 New Street
  Aylesbury
  Bucks HP20 2NW
  Tel: (0296) 4328861

The following hotels have specially adapted rooms in some of their hotels; Hotel Ibis, Hotel Mercure, Novotel and Hotel Sofitel. They can all be booked through the Resinter Hotel agency:

- **Resinter**
  1 Shortlands
  Hammersmith
  London W6 8DR
  Tel: 071-724 1000

Holidays with a difference

- **Youth Hostel Association**
  Trevalyan House
  8 St Stephens Hill
  St Albans
  Herts AL1 2DY
  Tel: (0727) 55215
- **Skill Share Africa**
  Ceresole House
  53 Regent Road
  Leicester LE1 6YL
  Tel: (0533) 541862
- **Quaker International**
  Friends House
  Euston Road
  London NW1 2BJ
  Tel: 071-387 3601
- **Camping for the Disabled**
  20 Burton Close
  Dawley
  Telford
  Shropshire TF4 2BX
  Tel: (0952) 507653 evenings only
  SAE with all enquiries
- **The Camping and Caravanning Club**
  11 Lower Grosvenor Place
  London SW1W OEY
  Tel: 071-828 1012
- **The Forestry Commission - Publications**
  231 Corstorphine Road
  Edinburgh EH12 7AT
  Tel: 031-334 0303

TRAVEL AIDS: SUPPLIERS' ADDRESSES

Signs and signals

- **Disabled Drivers' Association**
  Help pennant
  Ashwellthorpe
  Norwich NR16 1EX
  Tel: (050 841) 449
- **F Llewellyn Ltd**
  Sliding boards
  Regent House
  Regent Road
  City
  Liverpool L3 7BX
  Tel: 051-236 5311

Back rests

- **Aremco**
  Posture back support
  Grove House
  Lenham
  Kent ME17 2PX
  Tel: (0622) 858502
- **Health and Comfort**
  PO Box 15
  Westbury
  Wilts BA13 4GS
  Tel: (0373) 822394
- **Huntleigh Medical Ltd**
  Dorison foam, water and sheepskin cushions for wheelchairs and motorists
  Dallow Road
  Luton LU1 1UU
  Tel: (0582) 413104
- **Joncare Ltd**
  Body, wedge and cushion supports for own chair
  7 Ashville Trading Estate
  Nuffield Way
  Abingdon
  Oxon OX14 1RL
  Tel: (0235) 28120
- **M & F Systems**
  Insulated gel/foam cusion
  35-37 Grosvenor Road
  Aldershot
  Hants GU11 3DP
  Tel: (0252) 29551
- **Antler Ltd (Plastics Division)**
  Seabird medical cushion self-adjustable to take weight
  Western Way
  Exeter EX1 2AA
  Tel: (0392) 51002
- **Spenco Medical Ltd**
  Omega Dermal cushion
  Burrell Road
  Haywards Heath
  West Sussex RH16 1TW
  Tel: (0444) 415171

Hoists

- **S Burville & Son**
  Burville car top hydraulic hoist
  39 Primrose Road
  Hersham
  Walton on Thames
  Surrey
  Tel: (0932) 227454
- **Haltract Ltd**
  Haltract Midget Hoists operated by pulley system
  119-123 Sandycombe Road
  Richmond
  Surrey TW9 2ER
  Tel: 081-940 3322
- **Arjo-Mecanaids Ltd**
  Mecalift mobile, free-standing, mechanically operated hoist
  St Catherines Street
  Gloucester GL1 2SL
  Tel: (0452) 500200
- **Wessex Medical Equipment**
  Wessex Mobile Lifter, also small electric car hoist which runs off car battery
  Romsey
  Hampshire
  Tel: (0794) 83030

Seat belts/harnesses

- **Crelling Harnesses for the Disabled**
  range of quick-release harnesses
  11 The Crescent
  Cleveleys
  Lancs FY5 3LJ
  Tel: (0253) 852298

- **EDTS Ltd**
  harnesses made to individual requirements, individually made adapted car seats
  Highfields Works
  West Byfleet Corner
  West Byfleet
  Surrey KT14 5LP
  Tel: (09323) 42043

Car seating

- **D G Hodge & Son**
  sliding, swivelling replacement seat
  Feathers Lane
  Hythe End
  Wraysbury
  Staines
  Middlesex
  Tel: (0753) 683580

USEFUL ADDRESSES FOR ESSENTIAL AIDS

- **British Red Cross Society**
  9 Grosvenor Crescent
  London SW1X 7EJ
  Tel: 071-235 5454

- **Disabled Living Foundation (DLF)**
  380/384 Harrow Road
  London NW9 2HU
  Tel: 071-289 6111

- **The Joint Aid Centres Council**
  76 Clarendon Park Road
  Leicester LE2 3AD
  Tel: (0533) 700 747
  (for addresses of venues of travelling aids exhibitions)

NATIONAL TOURIST OFFICES

ANTIGUA

Antigual National Tourist Office
15 Thayer Street
London W1
Tel: 071-486 7073

AUSTRALIA

Australian Tourist Commission
Gemini House
10-18 Putney Hill
London SW15 6AA
Tel: 081-780 1424
081-780 2227 (Guide for disabled travellers)

AUSTRIA

Austrian National Tourist Office
30 St George Street
London W1R 9FA
Tel: 071-629 0461
General information plus leaflet ***Austrian Hotel Guide for Disabled Persons*** which lists suitable hotels.

BAHAMAS

Bahamas Ministry of Tourism
10 Chesterfield Street
London W1X 8AH
Tel: 071-629 5238
General information plus sheet ***Facilities for the Physically Disabled*** which lists suitable hotels.

BARBADOS

Barbados National Tourist Office
1 Tottenham Court Road
London W1
Tel: 071-636 9448
(Sandy Beach Hotel has facilities for disabled visitors)

BELGIUM

Belgium Tourist Office
Premier House
2 Gayton Road
Harrow
Middlesex HA1 2XU
Tel: 081-861 3300

BERMUDA

Department of Tourism
1 Battersea Church Road
London SW11 3LY
Tel: 071-734 8813/4
General information and information sheet ***Handicapped Visitors - Facilities in Bermuda*** which lists suitable hotels, transport, shopping and places of interest.

BRAZIL

Brazilian Embassy
32 Green Street
London W1Y 4AT
Tel: 071-499 0877
(between 3.30-5.30pm Tourist Desk)

BULGARIA

Bulgarian National Tourist Office
18 Princes Street
London W1R 7RE
Tel: 071-499 6988

CANADA

Commercial Division, Tourism
Canada House
Trafalgar Square
London SW1Y 5BJ
Tel: 071-629 9490
071-930 8540

CAYMAN ISLANDS

Cayman Islands Department of Tourism
Hambleton House
197 Knightsbridge
London SW7
Tel: 071-581 9960

CHINA

China National Tourist Office
4 Glentworth Street
London NW1
Tel: 071-935 9427

CUBA

Cuban Embassy
15 Grape Street
London WC2
Tel: 071-836 7618
071-240 2488
(Write for specialist travel information)

CYPRUS

Cyprus Tourism Organisation
213 Regent Street
London W1R 8DA
Tel: 071-734 9822
General information and information sheet ***What the Disabled Visitor needs to know about Cyprus*** which lists some suitable hotels.

CZECHOSLOVAKIA

Czechoslovakia Travel Bureau
17/18 Old Bond Street
London W1X 3DA
Tel: 071-629 6058

DENMARK

Danish Tourist Board
Sceptre House
169/173 Regent Street
London W1R 8PY
Tel: 071-734 2637
General information plus 119 page booklet ***Access in Denmark - A Tourist Guide for the Disabled*** which includes information on transport, accommodation, restaurants, places of interest etc.

EGYPT

Egyptian State Tourist Office
168 Piccadilly
London W1V 9DE
Tel: 071-493 5282/3
General information and information sheet ***Special Services for the Aged and Disabled*** which includes details of suitable hotels.

FIJI

Fiji National Tourist Office
Suite 33
High Holborn House
52/54 High Holborn
London WC1V 6RB
Tel: 071-242 3131

FINLAND

Finnish Tourist Office
Queens House
66/68 Haymarket
London SW1Y 4RF
Tel: 071-839 4048
(9.15am-12 noon weekdays)
The Finnish Tourist Office issue a comprehensive 168-page ***Finland Handbook*** which gives general information and also uses the International Access Symbol in the Hotel section to denote suitability for disabled visitors.

FRANCE

French Government Tourist Office
178 Piccadilly
London W1V OAL
Tel: 071-491 7622

071-499 6911 (recorded message)
General information plus information sheet ***Disabled Visitors to France*** which gives addresses of contact organisations.

THE GAMBIA

Gambian High Commission
57 Kensington Court
London W8 5DG
Tel: 071-937 6316

EAST GERMANY

Berolina Travel Ltd
22 Conduit Street
London W1R 9TD
Tel: 071-629 1664
General information but no specific information for disabled visitors. Suggests 5 star de-luxe hotels in major cities have limited facilities.

WEST GERMANY

German National Tourist Office
61 Conduit Street
London W1R OEN
Tel: 071-734 2600
General information plus fact sheet ***Information for the Disabled Visitor to the Federal Republic of Germany*** which gives contact addresses for accessible accommodation and some general information.

GIBRALTAR

Gibraltar Government Tourist Office
Arundel Great Court
179 The Strand
London WC2R 1EH
Tel: 071-836 0777

GREECE

National Tourist Organisation of Greece
4 Conduit Street
London W1R ODJ
Tel: 071-734 5997
General information and information sheet ***Hotels with facilities for Handicapped People***.

HONG KONG

Hong Kong Tourist Association
125 Pall Mall
London SW1Y 5EA
Tel: 071-930 4775
General information plus leaflet ***A Guide for Physically Handcapped Visitors to Hong Kong*** which lists accessible facilities at the airport, places of interest and hotels.

HUNGARY

Hungarian National Tourist Office
Danube Travel Agency
6 Conduit Street
London W1
Tel: 071-493 0263
General information but no specific information for disabled travellers.

ICELAND

Iceland Tourist Information Bureau
3rd Floor
172 Tottenham Court Road
London W1P 9LG
Tel: 071-499 9971/2
081-388 5346

INDIA

Government of India Tourist Office
7 Cork Street
London W1X 9DD
Tel: 071-437 3677/8
General information plus comprehensive hotel and restaurant guide. Suggests most 4 and 5 star hotels have facilities for disabled visitors.

INDONESIA

Indonesian Express
70/71 New Bond Street
London W1Y 9DE
Tel: 071-491 4469

ISRAEL

Israel Government Tourist Office
18 Great Marlborough Street
London W1V 1AF
Tel: 071-434 3651

ITALY

Italian State Tourist Office
1 Princes Street
London W1R 8AY
Tel: 071-408 1254

JAMAICA

Jamaica Tourist Board
111 Gloucester Place
London W1H 3PH
Tel: 071-493 3647
071-224 0505
General information plus information sheet ***Hotels with Facilities to assist the Physically Handicapped***.

JAPAN

Japan National Tourist Organisation
167 Regent Street
London W1R 7FD
Tel: 071-734 9638

JORDAN

Jordan National Tourist Office
211 Regent Street
London W1
Tel: 071-437 9465
(Printed matter available for disabled travellers).

KENYA

Kenya National Tourist Office
13 New Burlington Street
London W1X 1FF
Tel: 071-839 4477
071-355 3144

SOUTH KOREA

Korean National Tourist Corporation
Vogue House
1 Hanover Square
London W1R 9RD
Tel: 071-408 1591

LUXEMBOURG

Luxenbourg National Tourist & Trade Office
36/37 Piccadilly
London W1V 9PA
Tel: 071-434 2800
General information plus hotel guide which uses international wheelchair symbol to indicate those suitable for disabled visitors.

MACAU

Macau Tourist Information Bureau
22 Devonshire Street
London W1N 1RL
Tel: 071-629 6828
071-224 3390

MALAYSIA

Malaysian Tourist Office
57 Trafalgar Square
London WC2N 5DU
Tel: 071-499 7388
071-930 7932

MALTA

Malta National Tourist Office
Mappin House
Suite 300
4 Wisley Street
London W1N 7AR
Tel: 071-323 0506

MAURITIUS

Mauritius Government Office
49 Conduit Street
London W1
Tel: 071-437 7508
The Mauritius Government Tourist Office can recommend hotels that are convenient for holidaymakers in wheelchairs and also provide general information.

MEXICO

Mexican Government Tourist Office
60-91 Trafalgar Square
London WC2N 5DS
Tel: 071-734 1058/9

MONACO

Monaco Government Tourist & Convention Office
25 Whitehall
London SW1A 2BS
Tel: 071-930 4699

MOROCCO

Moroccan National Tourist Office
174 Regent Street
London W1R 6HB
Tel: 071-437 0073

NETHERLANDS

Netherlands Board of Tourism
25-28 Buckingham Gate
London SW1E 9LD
Tel: 071-630 0451
General information plus booklet ***Holiday and recreational opportunities for the physically disabled*** which lists suitable accommodation, restaurants, petrol stations with adapted toilets, places of interest etc.

NEW ZEALAND

New Zealand Tourist Office
New Zealand House
Haymarket
London SW1Y 4TQ
Tel: 071-930 8422

NORWAY

Norwegian Tourist Board
Charles House
5 Lower Regent Street
London SW1Y 4LR
Tel: 071-839 2650
General information plus booklet ***Availability of Overnight Accommodation in Norway in establishments suitable for the Physically Handicapped***.

PAKISTAN

Information Division
36 Lowndes Square
London SW1X 9JN
Tel: 071-235 2044

PERU

National Tourist Office of Peru
10 Grosvenor Gardens
London SW1
Tel: 071-824 8693

PHILIPPINES

National Tourist Office of the Philippines
199 Piccadilly
London W1V 9LE
Tel: 071-439 3481

POLAND

Polish Travel Lines
154 Cromwell Road
London SW7 4EF
Tel: 071-370 6131

PORTUGAL

Portuguese National Tourist Office
New Bond Street House
1/5 New Bond Street
London W1Y ONP
Tel: 071-493 3873
General information plus factsheet with contact list of main Portuguese institutions for disabled people.

ST KITTS, NEVIS, ST LUCIA, ST VINCENT, GRENADINES

East Caribbean Tourist Association
10 Kensington Court
London W8 5DL
Tel: 071-937 6570

SEYCHELLES

Seychelles Tourist Board
Fourth Floor
50 Conduit Street
London W1A 4PE
Tel: 071-439 0405
General information and suggestions for suitable hotels.

SINGAPORE

Singapore Tourist Board
1 Carrington House
126 Regent Street
London W1
Tel: 071-437 0033

SOVIET UNION

Intourist Moscow Ltd
292 Regent Street
London W1R
Tel: 071-631 1252
071-538 8600

SPAIN

Spanish National Tourist Office
57/58 St James's Street
London SW1A 1LD
Tel: 071-499 0901
General information plus fact sheet ***Information of interest to the Disabled***

which lists contact addresses and some hotels considered suitable.

SRI LANKA

Sri Lanka Tourist Board
London House
53-54 Haymarket
London SW1Y 4RP
Tel: 071-321 0034
071-242 3131

SWEDEN

Swedish National Tourist Office
3 Cork Street
London W1X 1HA
Tel: 071-437 5816
General information plus 149-page ***Holiday Guide for the Disabled*** which gives information on travel, transport, suitable accommodation, places of interest, etc.

SWITZERLAND

Swiss National Tourist Office
Swiss Centre
1 New Coventry Street
London W1V 8EE
Tel: 071-734 1921
General information plus booklet ***Swiss Hotel Guide for the Disabled*** which lists hotels suitable for disabled visitors.

TAIWAN

Free Chinese Centre
4th Floor
Dorland House
14/16 Regent Street
London SW1Y 4PH
Tel: 071-930 9553

THAILAND

Tourism Authority of Thailand
49 Albermarle Street
London W1X 3FE
Tel: 071-499 7679

TRINIDAD & TOBAGO

Tourist Board
48 Leicester Square
London WC2
Tel: 071-839 7155

TUNISIA

Tunisian Tourist Office
7a Stafford Street
London W1X 4EQ
Tel: 071-499 2234

TURKEY

The Turkish Tourist Office
Egyptian House
170/173 Piccadilly
London W1V 9DD
Tel: 071-734 8681

TURKS & CAICOS ISLANDS

West India Committee
48 Albermarle Street
London W1X 4AR
Tel: 071-629 6353
General information but no specific information for disabled visitors.

UNITED STATES

United States Travel & Tourism Administration
22 Sackville Street
London W1X 2EA
Tel: 071-439 7433

YUGOSLAVIA

Yugoslavia National Tourist Office
143 Regent Street
London W1R 8AE
Tel: 071-734 5243
General information plus the suggestion that disabled visitors stay at 'Health Spa' resorts which are located on the coast and offer facilities for disabled people. Brochure on Health Spas available from Tourist Office or for more information Mrs Nina Oberiter-Gluhak, 41000 Zagreb, c/o Hotel Jadran, Vlaska 50, Yugoslavia.

SPECIALIST COMPANIES WHO ARRANGE HOLIDAYS FOR DISABLED PEOPLE

- **Assistance Travel**
  1 Quarry View House
  Tank Lane
  Purfleet
  Essex RM16 1TA
  Tel: (0708) 963198
  Specialise in holidays in Florida and the UK but also offer tailor-made holidays worldwide for individuals and families with a disabled member.
- **Carefree Holidays Ltd**
  64 Florence Road
  Abingdon
  Northampton NN1 4NA
  Tel: (0604) 34301 or 330382
  Holidays for retired people and those with special needs in hotels and holiday centres. 20 per cent supplementary charge for helpers.
- **Chalfont Line**
  4 Meadway Parade
  Perivale
  Middlesex UB6 8HA
  Tel: 081-997 3799
  Group holidays in the UK and abroad using wheelchair-adapted coach.
- **Threshold Travel**
  80 Newry Street
  Banbridge
  Co. Down
  BT32 3HA
  Tel: (0820) 626267
  Holidays for groups and individual disabled travellers.

VOLUNTARY GROUPS WHO ARRANGE HOLIDAYS FOR DISABLED PEOPLE

- **The Disaway Trust**
  2 Charles Road
  Merton Park
  London SW19 3BD
  Tel: 081-543 3431
  Group holidays in the UK and abroad for disabled people.
- **Young Disabled on Holiday**
  33 Longfield Avenue
  Heald Green
  Cheadle
  Cheshire SK8 3NH
  Tel: 061-499 3639
  Group holidays in the UK and abroad for disabled people from 16-30 years.
- **John Grooms Association for the Disabled**
  10 Gloucester Drive
  Finsbury Park
  London N4 2LP
  Tel: 081-802 7272
  Adapted hotels and self-catering

accommodation. Also fully equipped narrow boat.

- **Mobility International**
  228 Borough High Street
  London SE1 1JX
  Tel: 071-403 5688
  Organises activities and conferences abroad for disabled and able-bodied young people.
- **PHAB**
  Tavistock House North
  Tavistock Square
  London WC1H 9HJ
  Tel: 071-388 1963
  Organises holidays and group activities in the UK and abroad for disabled and able-bodied young people.
- **Winged Fellowship Trust**
  Angel House
  Pentonville Road
  London NW1 9XD
  Tel: 071-833 2594
  Group holidays abroad and in the UK for disabled people.

Purpose-Built Accommodation Abroad

- Sue Abbot
  UK Agent -Mar Y Sol
  123 Copper Mill Road
  Wraysbury
  Staines
  Middlesex TW19 5NX
  Tel: (0753) 685718
  Mar Y Sol is a wheelchair-friendly holiday and health centre in Los Cristianos, Tenerife. Facilities include two swimming pools, one heated with pool hoist, restaurant, sauna, gymnasium, massage, hydrotherapy and other health treatments available. Wheelchair-accessible apartments and studios.

UK

- **Calvert Trust Adventure Centre**
  Little Crosthwaite
  Underskiddaw
  Keswick
  Cumbria CA12 4QD
  Tel: (07687) 72254
  The centre enables disabled people to enjoy a variety of outdoor activities in an area of outstanding beauty in the Lake District National Park.
- **Stackpole Trust**
  Goldborough Farm
  Hundleton
  Nr Pembroke
  Dyfed SA71 5RF
  Tel: (0646) 685929
  Holiday and study centre surrounded by farmland and situated close to the South Pembrokeshire National Park. Wheelchair-accessible beaches close by.

Some Useful Publications

- ***AA Guide for the Disabled Traveller***
  Automobile Association
  Fanum House
  Basingstoke
  Hants RG21 2EA
  Tel: (0256) 20123
  free to members
- ***The Disabled Traveller's International Phrase Book***
  The Disabled Press
  60 Greenhayes Avenue
  Banstead
  Surrey SM7 2JQ
- ***How ABTA Safeguards your Holiday***
  Association of British Travel Agents
- ***How to Help the Disabled Traveller***
  Consumer Relations Department
  55-57 Newman Street
  London W1P 4AH
  Tel: 071-637 2444
- ***Holiday and Travel Abroad - A Guide for Disabled People***
  RADAR
  25 Mortimer Street
  London W1N 8AB
  Tel: 071-637 5400
- ***Holidays for Disabled People UK***
  Address as above
- ***Low Cost Travel Tips for People Using Wheelchairs***
  Mobility International
  62 Union Street
  London SE1
  Tel: 071-403 5688
- ***Activity & Hobby Holidays***
  English Tourist Board
  4 Bromells Road
  Clapham Common
  London SW4 0BJ
  Tel: 081-846 9000

Conversion Charts Weights and Measures

LIQUID CONVERSION CHART

To convert gallons to litres
Read the centre column as gallons. The left hand column is the equivalent in litres

To convert litres to gallons
Read the centre column as litres. The right hand column is the equivalent in gallons

Litres		*Gallons*
4.546	**1**	0.22
9.092	**2**	0.44
13.638	**3**	0.66
18.184	**4**	0.88
22.730	**5**	1.10
27.276	**6**	1.32
31.822	**7**	1.54
36.368	**8**	1.76
40.914	**9**	1.98
45.460	**10**	2.20

When buying petrol, 4.5 litres is about equivalent to one gallon.

METRIC MEASURES AND EQUIVALENTS

Length

1 millimetre (mm)		= 0.0394 in
1 centimetre (cm)	= 10 mm	= 0.3937 in
1 metre (m)	= 100 cm	= 1.0936 yd
1 kilometre (km)	= 1000 m	= 0.6214 mile

To convert	*Multiply by*
millimetres to inches	0.0394
metres to feet	3.2808
metres to yards	1.0936
kilometres to miles	0.6214

Weight

1 gram (g)	= 1000 mg	= 0.0353 oz
1 kilogram (kg)	= 1000 g	= 2.2046 lb

To convert	*Multiply by*
grams to ounces	0.0353
grams to pounds	0.0022
kilograms to pounds	2.2046

ELECTRICAL EQUIPMENT

Most of the Continental countries use 220/240 volts AC so take an adaptor with you or wait until you arrive at your destination and check the type of socket available. A suitable plug/adaptor can then be obtained from a local electrical shop. Two-pin plugs are usually the rule on the Continent.

USEFUL WORDS AND PHRASES

Disability/disabled

French: Infirmite/infirme
German: Korperehindertheit/korperbehindert
Italian: L'invalidita/handicappato
Spanish: Invalidez/invalido
Portuguese: Deficiencia/deficiente
Swedish: Handikapp/handikappad
Dutch: Invalidteit/invalide, gehandicapte

Paralysed/paraplegic

French: Paralyse/paralytique
German: Gelahmt/Paraplegisch
Italian: Paralasi/paralitico
Spanish: Paralitico/paraplegico
Portuguese: Paralitico/paraplegico
Swedish: Forlamning/forlamad
Dutch: Verlamd/dwarslaesie

Swelling/swollen

French: Tumefaction/tumefie
German: Geschwulst/Geschwollen
Italian: Gonfiarsi/gonfiato
Spanish: Hinchazon/hinchado
Portuguese: Edema/inchado
Swedish: Svullnad/svullen
Dutch: Opzwellen/gezwollen

Glue

French: Colle
German: Leim
Italian: L'adesivo
Spanish: Goma de pegar
Portuguese: Cola
Swedish: Lim
Dutch: Gom

Analgaesic/pain killer

French: Analgesique/coupe-douleur
German: Betaubungsmittel/schmerzstillende Pulver
Italian: L'analgetico
Spanish: Analgesico/para quitar los dolores
Portuguese: Analgesico
Swedish: Smartstillande medel
Dutch: Pijnloosheid/pijnstiller

Urinal

French: Urinal
German: Harnflasche
Italian: L'orinale
Spanish: Orinal
Portuguese: Urinal
Swedish: Pissoar
Dutch: Urinaal

Hoist

French: Poulie, grue
German: Flaschenzug
Italian: L'apparecchio di sollevamento
Spanish: Montacargas
Portuguese: Elevador
Swedish: Block-talja
Dutch: Ophijsen

Board/plank

French: Planche
German: Brett/Planke
Italian: L'asse
Spanish: Tabla/tablon
Portuguese: Tabua/prancha
Swedish: Brada
Dutch: Plank

Bath/bathroom

French: Bain/salle de bains
German: Bad/Badezimmer
Italian: Bagno
Spanish: Bano/cuarto de bano
Portuguese: Banho/casa de banho
Swedish: Bad/badrum
Dutch: Bad/badkamer

Lavatory/toilet

French: Lavabo/wc
German: WC/Ankleidezimmer
Italian: Il gabinetto
Spanish: Lavabo/retrete
Portuguese: Retrete/toilete
Swedish: WC/toalett
Dutch: WC/toilet

Seat/cushion

French: Siege/coussin
German: Sitz/Polster
Italian: La sedia/il cuscino
Spanish: Asiento/cojin
Portuguese: Assento/almofada
Swedish: Sate, sits/dyna
Dutch: Zitten/kussen

Foot plate

French: Pose-pieds
German: FuBplatte
Italian: Il supporto per i piedi
Spanish: Estribo
Portuguese: descanso para o pe
Swedish: Fotstod
Dutch: Voetplaat

Brake

French: Freins
German: Bremse
Italian: I freni
Spanish: Freno
Portuguese: Travao
Swedish: Broms
Dutch: Rem

Handle

French: Poignee
German: Griff
Italian: Il manubrio
Spanish: Asidero
Portuguese: Manipulos de conducao
Swedish: Handtag
Dutch: Handvat

Fold/folding

French: Pli/pliage
German: Falten/Faltung
Italian: Pieghevole
Spanish: Piegado/plegable
Portuguese: Dobrar/dobravel
Swedish: Falla ihop/hopfallbar
Dutch: Samenklappen

Detachable

French: Detachable
German: Abnehmbar
Italian: Smontabile
Spanish: Desmontable
Portuguese: Desmontavel
Swedish: Avtagbar
Dutch: Afneembaar

Width

French: Largeur
German: Breite
Italian: Misura
Spanish: Ancho
Portuguese: Largura
Swedish: Bredd
Dutch: Breedte

Hospital

French: Hopital
German: Spital
Italian: L'ospedale
Spanish: Hospital
Portuguese: Hospital
Swedish: Sjukhus
Dutch: Ziekenhuis/hospitaal

Doctor

French: Medecin
German: Arzt
Italian: Il medico
Spanish: Doctor
Portuguese: Medico
Swedish: Lakare
Dutch: Dokter

Chemist

French: Pharmacien
German: Apotheke
Italian: La farmacia
Spanish: Farmaceutico
Portuguese: Farmacia
Swedish: Apotak
Dutch: Apotheker

Telephone

French: Telephone
German: Telefon
Italian: Il telefono
Spanish: Telefono
Portuguese: Telefone
Swedish: Telefon
Dutch: Telefoon

Wheelchair

French: Fauteuil roulant
German: Rollstuhl
Italian: La sedia a rotelle
Spanish: Silla de ruedas
Portuguese: Cadeiras de rodas
Swedish: Rullstol
Dutch: Rolstoel

Push!

French: Poussez!
German: Drucken!
Italian: Spinga!
Spanish: Empujad!
Portuguese: Empurre!
Swedish: Skjut!
Dutch: Duwen!

Lift!

French: Levez!
German: Heben!
Italian: Sollevi!
Spanish: Levantad!
Portuguese: Levante!
Swedish: Lyft!
Dutch: Tillen!

Stop!

French: Stop!
German: Stop!
Italian: Alt!
Spanish: Alto!
Portuguese: Pare!
Swedish: Stopp!
Dutch: Stop/halt!

Let Go!

French: Lachez!
German: Auslassen!
Italian: Lasci andare!
Spanish: Soltar!
Portuguese: Largue!
Swedish: Slapp!
Dutch: Loslaten!

USEFUL PHRASES

Are there any steps/stairs?

French: Y-a-t'il des marches/des escaliers?
German: Sind hier Stufen/Stiegen?
Italian: Ci sono dei gradini/delle scale?
Spanish: Hay escalones/escaleras?
Portuguese: Ha ali degraus/escadas?
Swedish: Finns det nagra trappsteg/trappor?
Dutch: Zijn er opstapjes/trappen?

Is there a ramp/slope?

French: Y-a-t'il une rampe de montee/un plan incline?
German: Ist dort eine Auffahrt/ein Hugel?
Italian: C'e una rampa?
Spanish: Hay una rampa/un terraplen?
Portuguese: Ha uma rampa/declive?
Swedish: Finns det ramp?
Dutch: Is er een helling/loopt het schuin af?

How many steps are there?

French: Combien de marches y-a-t'il?
German: Wieviele Stufen sind dort?
Italian: Quanti sono i gradini?
Spanish: Cuantos escalones hay?
Portuguese: Quantos degraus ha?
Swedish: Hur manga trappsteg ar det?
Dutch: Hoe veel treden zijn er?

Is there an entrance without steps?

French: Y-a-t'il une entree sans marches?
German: Gibt es einen Eingang ohne Stufen?
Italian: C'e una entrata senza gradini?
Spanish: Hay alguna entrado sin escalones?
Portuguese: Ha uma entrada sem degraus?
Swedish: Finns det en ingang utan trappsteg?
Dutch: Is er een ingang zonder treden?

Where is the nearest toilet?

French: Ou se trouve le wc le plus proche?
German: Wo ist der Nachste WC?
Italian: Dove sono i gabinetti?
Spanish: Donde estan los lavabos?
Portuguese: Onde e a toilete/casa de banho mais perto?
Swedish: Var ar narmasta toallet?
Dutch: Waar is de dichtsbijzijnde toilet?

Have you a room suitable for a person in a wheelchair?

French: Avez-vous une chambre appropriee a une infirme dans un fauteuil roulant?
German: Haben Sie ein Geeignetes Zimmer Fur Einen Korperbehinderten mit Rollstuhl?
Italian: Ha una stanza adatta per una persona in sedia a rotelle?
Spanish: Tiene usted una habitacion adecuada para una persona en silla de ruedas?
Portuguese: Tem um quarto adequado para uma pessoa em cadeira de rodas?
Swedish: Har ni ett rum som passar for en person i rullstol?
Dutch: Heeft U een kamer geschikt voor een rolstoel gebruiker?

Are the doors wide enough for a wheelchair?

French: Les portes sont-elles suffusamment larges pour laisser passer un fauteuil roulant?
German: Sind die Turen breit genug fur einen Rollstuhl?
Italian: Le porte sono abbastanza larghe per una sedia a rotelle?
Spanish: Son las puertas bastante anchas para una silla de ruedas?
Portuguese: Tem as portas a largura suficiente para uma cadeira de rodas?
Swedish: Ar dorrarna breda nog for en rullstol?
Dutch: Zihn de deuren breed genoeg voor een rolstoel?

My wheelchair is ... cms wide

French: Mon fauteuil roulant a une largeur de ... cms
German: Mein Rollstuhl ist ... cma breit
Italian: Mia sedia a rotelle ha ... cm di larghezza
Spanish: Mi silla de ruedas tiene un ancho de ... cms
Portuguese: Minha cadeira de rodas tem ... cms de largura
Swedish: Min rullstol ar ... cm bred
Dutch: Mijn rolstoel is ... cm breed

Please put my wheelchair in the car

French: Veuillez mettre mon fauteuil roulant dans la voiture
German: Bitte tragen Sie meinen Rollstuhl in das Auto
Italian: Per favore, mette la sedia nella macchina
Spanish: Haga el favor de poner la silla de ruedas en el coche
Portuguese: Por favor ponha a cadeira de rodas no carro
Swedish: Var snall och stall rullstolen i bilen
Dutch: Wilt U mijn rolstoel in de auto doen?

May I travel/stay in my wheelchair?

French: Puis-je voyager/rester dans mon fauteuil roulant?
German: Kann ich mit Rollstuhl reisen/in meinem Rollstuhl sitzenbleiben?
Italian: Posso restare nella mia sedia durante il viaggio?
Spanish: Puedo ir/quedarme en la silla de ruedas?
Portuguese: Posso viajar/ficar na cadeira de rodas?
Swedish: Kan jag sitta kvar i min rullstol?
Dutch: Mag ik in mijn rolstoel reizen/in mijn rolstoel blijven zitten?

My car has broken down. Where is the nearest garage?

French: Ma voiture est en panne. Ou est le garage le plus proche?
German: Mein Auto hat eine Panne. Wo ist die nachste Werkstatt?
Italian: La mia macchina e guasta. Dov'e l'officina piu vicina?
Spanish: Mi coche esta estropeado. Cual es el garje mas proximo?
Portuguese: O meu carro avariou-se. Onde fica a oficina mais proxima?
Swedish: Min bil gar inte. Var ar narmaste bilverkstad?
Dutch: Mijn auto is stuk. Waar is de dichsbijzijnde garage?

I have a disabled passenger

French: J'ai un passager infirme
German: Ich habe einen korperbehinderten Mitfahrer
Italian: Ho con me un viaggiatore handicappato
Spanish: Tengo un pasajero invalido
Portuguese: Eu tenho um passageiro deficiente
Swedish: Jag har en invalidiserad passagerare
Dutch: Ik heb een gehandicapte passagier

The battery needs recharging

French: La batterie a besoin d'etre rechargee
German: Die Batterie muss aufgeladen werden
Italian: Occorre ricaricare la batteria
Spanish: Hace falta cargar la bateria
Portuguese: E Preciso carregar a bateria
Swedish: Batteriet behover laddas om
Dutch: De accu moet opgeladen

I am disabled/a disabled driver

French: Je suis infirme/un conducteur infirme
German: Ich bin korperbehindert/ein korperbehindert Fahrer
Italian: Sono handicappato(a)/sono un automobilista handicappato
Spanish: Estoy invalido/un conductor invalido
Portuguese: Eu sou um deficiente/um condutor deficiente
Swedish: Jag ar handikappad/en handikappad forare
Dutch: Ik ben gehamndicapt/een gehandicapte bestuurder

I cannot walk up steps/stairs

French: Je ne peux pas monter les marches/les escaliers
German: Ich kann nicht die stufen/stiegen hinaufgehan
Italian: Non posso salire i gradini/le scale
Spanish: No puedo subir escalones/escaleras
Portuguese: Nao posso subir degraus/escadas
Swedish: Jag kan inte ga upp for trappsteg/trappor
Dutch: Ik lam niet geen opstapje doen/trappen lopen

Can you/someone please help me?

French: Pouvez-vous/quelqu'un peut-il m'aider?
German: Konnen Sie mir/kann mir bitte jemand helfen?
Italian: C'e qualcuno che potrebbe aiutarme?
Spanish: Puede usted/puede alguien ayudarme, por favor?
Portuguese: Pode voce/alguem ajudar-me, por favor?
Swedish: Kan ni/nagon vara vanlig och hjalpa mig?
Dutch: Kunt U/kan iemand mij helpen?

May I have a/another pillow/blanket please?

French: Puis-je avoir un coussin/une couverture supplementaire?
German: Kann ich bitte noch einen Polster/eine Deck haben?
Italian: Posso avere un cuscino/soperte in piu?
Spanish: Me puede dar otra almohada/manta, por favor?
Portuguese: Posso ter uma/outra almofada/covertor, por favor?
Swedish: Kan jag fa en/ytterligare en kudde/filt?
Dutch: Mag ij een/nog een kussen/nog een deken?

Please cut this up for me

French: Pourriez-vous me couper ceci
German: Bitte schneiden Sie dies fur mich
Italian: Per favore, metta via questo/quello
Spanish: Haga el favor de cortamelo
Portuguese: Por favor corte-me isto
Swedish: Var vanlig skar upp detta at mig
Dutch: Wilt U/dit voor mij open snijden

Can you please help me across this road/up this/these steps?

French: Pourriez-vous m'aider a traverser la rue/a monter cette/ces marche(s)?
German: Wurden Sie mir bitte uber die Strasse/diese(n) Stufe(n) halfen?
Italian: Potrebbe aiutarmi ad attraversare questa strada/questo gradino?
Spanish: Me puede ayudar, por favor, a vruzar la calle/subir los escalones?
Portuguese: Pode ajudar-me a atravessar esta rua/subir este/estes degraus?
Swedish: Vill ni hjalpa mig over gatan/upp for trappan/trapporna?
Dutch: Wilt U mij helpen oversteken/hierop helpen/bij deze treden?